The Soulwork of Clay

A Hands-On Approach to Spirituality

Marjory Zoet Bankson

Photographs by Peter Bankson

Walking Together, Finding the Way ®
SKYLIGHT PATHS ®
PUBLISHING

The Soulwork of Clay: A Hands-On Approach to Spirituality

For information regarding permission to reprint material from this book, please mail or fax your request in writing to SkyLight Paths Publishing, Permissions Department, at the address / fax number listed below or e-mail your request to permissions@skylightpaths.com.

Grateful acknowledgment is given for permission to use the following material: Page 151, "Damp Smoking Pot (figure 7-1)," by Amy Curry, © Amy Curry. Photograph by Amy Curry. Used by permission.

Library of Congress Cataloging-in-Publication Data

Bankson, Marjory Zoet.
   The soulwork of clay : a hands-on approach to spirituality / Marjory Zoet Bankson ; photographs by Peter Bankson.—Paperback ed.
      p. cm.
   Includes index.
   ISBN-13: 978-1-59473-249-2 (quality pbk.)
   ISBN-10: 1-59473-249-3 (quality pbk.)
   1. Pottery craft. 2. Spirituality in art. I. Title.
   TT920.B3523 2008
   738.1'4—dc22

                                                                    2008038089

ISBN-13: 978-1-68336-301-9 (hc)
Manufactured in the United States of America
Cover design: Jenny Buono

SkyLight Paths Publishing is creating a place where people of different spiritual traditions come together for challenge and inspiration, a place where we can help each other understand the mystery that lies at the heart of our existence.

SkyLight Paths sees both believers and seekers as a community that increasingly transcends traditional boundaries of religion and denomination—people wanting to learn from each other, *walking together, finding the way.*

SkyLight Paths, "Walking Together, Finding the Way," and colophon are trademarks of LongHill Partners, Inc., registered in the U.S. Patent and Trademark Office.

Walking Together, Finding the Way®
Published by SkyLight Paths Publishing
An Imprint of Turner Publishing Company
4507 Charlotte Avenue, Suite 100
Nashville, TN 37209
Tel: (615) 255-2665
www.skylightpaths.com

For my Dutch grandmother,
Flossina Zeberdina Zoet,
and my father,
August G. Zoet
who taught me that handwork is a sacred art.

Contents

Acknowledgments

Without my husband, Peter, this book would not have been born. I took to clay in his absence. Then, for years, we lived on soups and bread because I worked at home, in a basement studio, and could keep an eye on the stove without fussing in the kitchen much. He was my comforter and cheerleader when the writing started, and then, when we decided to add the practical exercises, he took all the pictures in this book. Thank you, Peter, for your keen eye and quick wit all these years.

Marcia Broucek has been midwife, editor, and friend throughout the writing process. She asked questions to help me say what my hands knew how to do without thinking. She saw possibilities when I came to a wall, and she believed in my inner journey when I grew bashful before the computer screen.

My thanks, too, to Jean and Louie Mideke who opened their home and their lives to me when Peter was in Vietnam. As a professional potter, Louie never sought recognition or acclaim. It was enough for him to make classic, single-fired porcelain pots with local glazes that he developed himself. Several of them are pictured in this book as a way of naming him publicly for the artist/craftsman that he was. Jean was a fine jeweler who made our wedding rings, and she taught fifth grade for many years to provide them a regular income. Together they grew most of their own food, traveled widely through books from the public library, and grew orchids for their beauty in the wintertime. They were both models and mentors for me.

M. C. Richards blessed me with her writing, and later her friendship, as we explored spirituality and clay together. We first met at Pendle Hill, a Quaker retreat center outside of Philadelphia. I felt honored to walk with her more closely in the last few years of her life.

I also need to thank the many people who have come to my retreats over the years, to explore their own spirituality through art. Most of the exercises in this book were shared with retreatants who didn't know they were created to be creators, but who dared to get their hands in the mud. You gave me the response I needed to believe we could find language for those longings that we all have— to let the earth shape us even as our fingers create something new from the earth itself.

Prologue

I came to clay in a time of crisis. My husband had just been sent to Vietnam with the U.S. Army, and I was consumed by fear that he would not return the same man. I had gone back to my childhood home, in Bellingham, Washington, where I had begun a new job teaching seventh grade. But my heart was sick with dread and somehow the easy answers of "having faith" did nothing to relieve my fears.

A family friend, Louie Mideke, offered to let me use his "therapy wheel" in the evenings after he had finished work in his pottery studio for the day. I jumped at the chance. I had always wanted to try my hand with clay but had been caught up in more academic pursuits. Now, what had seemed to be a terrible emptiness in my life became an opportunity. I had time in the evenings, no ongoing social commitments, and a yearning to be productive in a physical way. I also hoped that I could learn to make beautiful pots ... but I knew that would take time and practice.

We began simply. I came to watch him throw with the intention of doing it myself. That changed the way I observed—with my whole being instead of just my eyes. He gave me a small piece of clay to hold and work while I watched, and something magical began to happen. It felt like my fingers were waking up from a long sleep. Then my hands and arms and shoulders quickened, even though I was not yet working at the potter's wheel myself. Over the next few months, I went to the studio more and more often.

Louie was a fine teacher because he left me alone with the clay. "I'm in the house if you have questions," he said. Louie's classic pots were all around the studio, drying from his day's work. His books were available, so I tried to read and learn what I could that way. I would usually work all evening in silence, then have a cup of tea with Louie and his wife, Jean, before going home. Often there was no question, just a quiet sense of their encouragement.

The clay was my primary teacher, as I reconnected with the mud-loving child in me. Clay brought me home to my body and to the earth itself. I noticed my breathing, my sense of what to do, my frustrations, problems solved or not, and ultimately, my sense of peace as I cleaned up each evening. Feelings surfaced. Something that had been split apart was healing in me. Looking back now, I know that my soul had found its home in the pottery studio.

One night, not long after I began working with clay, I had a dream of standing at my potter's wheel in a long line of potters, each one different but all engaged in making simple vessels for use by others. The line stretched back, and back, through time. I felt a sense of community with other potters over the centuries. I knew then that this journey was not just about my own solace or skill, but that I was part of something much larger: a tradition of artisans who made functional ware for human use. The dream gave me a sense that working with clay was taking me to a realm of connection, not only with previous generations, but with the earth itself.

Jean and Louie Mideke encouraged that sense of connection by the way they lived. He was largely self-taught as a potter and made most of his own tools. She was a jeweler who taught fifth grade with a strong focus on art. They had a large garden that supplied food. They were the only people I knew who subscribed to *The New Yorker*, *Scientific American*, and *Nature* magazines and made regular trips to the library for books. They grew orchids "for color in the winter." Louie kept careful records of his glaze experiments and was willing to share whatever I asked about, but he didn't burden me with too much information. He let my questions be our guide.

During that year, someone gave me a copy of M. C. Richards's book *Centering: In Pottery, Poetry, and the Person*. It gave me language for what I was feeling and assured me that I had entered into a realm of soulwork with good company. A decade later, I would attend a workshop with M. C. at Pendle Hill, a Quaker retreat center near Philadelphia, and we would begin a personal friendship that lasted until her death in 1999. But then, in the mid-sixties, it was her stream-of-consciousness writing that gave me the poetic language for what was awakening. "It is not the pots we are forming," she wrote, "but ourselves."

Yes, I thought. That's right. I am being formed by the clay. I am reconnecting with the earth, and with the other basic elements, too—air, water, fire —and life itself. Working with clay is so tactile and tangible, so immediate. Every gesture leaves its trail in the clay. Every fingerprint, a message. My breath fills the cavity. My touch curves the wall of a bowl. And inwardly, I am being formed by the outward practice. I am learning to trust the process, to lean into the possibilities rather than strive for some predetermined goal. I am being hollowed out, stretched and constricted, trimmed and sometimes reworked entirely.

Peter returned safely from Vietnam, and we spent the next year in Hanover, New Hampshire, before he returned for a second tour of duty. That time, I stayed in place to work in the dean's office at Dartmouth as a women's counselor, and to work for the League of New Hampshire Craftsmen as a shop steward, firing other people's pots in return for use of the pottery studio. By then, clay was becoming more than a nighttime diversion. I was beginning to feel the possibility of giving my full attention to the soulwork of clay. I had gained enough skill to sell my pots in the marketplace, but the real challenge was an inner one: to name the elements of story that were beginning to emerge.

SOULWORK

Soulwork is heartwork. It is the reunion of body and spirit, the connecting point of the lower chakras and the upper ones. It is linked with the aliveness and consciousness that we carry in our bodies. More than personality or character, soulwork speaks of personhood and humanity. Loving and longing. What we are here for. We hear this resonance in familiar phrases such as "soul food" or "soul music." Singing the blues. Sharing our heartaches. Soulwork is a process of joining the inward and outward dimensions of our lives that takes a lifetime.

Until I began working with clay, I had lost the connection between my cerebral thinking side and my physical self. I completely identified myself with my mind and was vaguely fearful of my reliably healthy body. Unfortunately, that separation is encouraged by our culture because we make better consumers if we are unconsciously split between body and spirit, focused on "things," having many choices to make. By contrast, clay is utterly simple. Completely available. Without artifice or artistry. It's just mud. And to let go of my pretensions in order to get my hands dirty and play "as a little child," I had to go back to a time when my spirit was utterly united with my body, and begin there. From that unconscious state of fusion, clay gave me a path to more conscious wholeness—feeling and thought, intuition and sensation—which is essential to soulwork.

In the forty years since my first exposure to clay, I have spent a decade as a professional potter, truly learning my craft. Then I moved in more theological circles as a seminary student, and later, as president of Faith at Work, a small-group relational ministry and magazine. More recently, I have returned to the pottery studio with a new call to create unfired burial urns for local clients (because they do not ship well). All the while, I have been writing about the mysterious process of discovery that comes from working with clay.

Now, as the ecological crisis looms in many forms, I feel a new urgency for finding ways that we can rediscover how much we love the earth itself. I believe this is the path for recovering our humanity, our sense of community with each other, and communion with all living things, especially air and water. While some people will go on a vision quest or a wilderness journey to reclaim this elemental sense of connection, I believe that working with clay (and other forms of handwork) can do the same thing at home.

Won't you join me in the journey of discovery that is the soulwork of clay? As a reminder to pause and wonder, each chapter contains reflective questions that can be done alone or shared with a small group of friends. At the end of each chapter, there are lots of clay projects for you to try. Have fun! This is a hands-on experience of the spiritual journey.

1
Grounding
The Basic Elements

Each morning, I sit quietly, holding a small ball of clay.
Eyes closed, my fingers explore the clay.
Slow movement rides on the rhythm of my breath.
I am one with the clay.

Call it morning prayer, or an unconscious union with our beginnings; holding a piece of soft clay is full of potential and possibility. Spontaneous movement begins to change its shape. Breath and body merge to begin a slow dance of new creation.

Because it is so available and so squeezable, clay invites an immediate body response as no other medium does. Children everywhere reach for the mud in creek beds or roadside puddles to squish out a shape and delight in what their hands have made. We are, even in this technological time, not only toolmakers who make things for necessity, but also artists who make things for the sheer joy of personal expression. At some level, we are all born to be artisans, to make things we can use or simply delight in—a magical thing, a tiny cup, a thumbprint that is "mine alone," an expression of self.

I once heard opera singer Beverly Sills say, "A craftsman needs to know how a thing will turn out, an artist does not." In that sense, every parent is both craftsman and artist: We want to know that our children will turn out well, and we cannot be sure that will happen. We all live in the tension of wanting predictable results, yet being bored by that. The body wants safety and security; the soul wants adventure, excitement, imagination. Our souls long to dance and sing and play without finite consequences. As a result, we live in the now and the not yet, the reality of what is and the possibility that our dreams can reach for.

Sitting quietly with a piece of soft clay can put us in touch with the whole story of creation and, at the same time, our soul's longing to participate as an artist, creating something new and unique. Working with clay becomes a way to express the soul's longing for life and love, even as we slip into an age of purchased substitutes for handmade things.

The clay journey begins with the raw elements of stone, water, and slime.

STONE

Clay begins as natural stone, some volcanically melted combination of alumina and silica that is hard and opaque. The mineral content varies throughout the earth, resulting in local differences of color and texture. In every piece of clay, we can feel the earth's crust as the original fireball cooled. Stone speaks of longevity (if not eternity) and of solidity and durability. The gritty, grainy substance of clay comes from igneous rock, usually some kind of feldspar. Some clay has a high silica content that, when the organic matter has been fired away, will ring like fine crystal. Other clay has a low silica content, which lets water percolate through a looser molecular structure.

Something in stone speaks to us, calls to us from beaches or mountain hikes. We respond to its color or smoothness, geologic age or striking contrast with surrounding turf. Because stones occur everywhere, we are not apt to regard them as precious artifacts. Instead, we pick them up and carry them home as reminders of a special time and place.

The Nature of Stones

- Before you continue reading, look around your house for stones you might have collected. Do you have any stones sitting on a windowsill? Clustered on your desk or in a fish tank? We frequently bring these back from trips, from special events, or simply because we are unconsciously drawn to gather stones.

- Take a few minutes to recall the places your stones represent—or simply to admire their beauty. Is there some common thread that runs through your collection? Something you love about these particular stones?

- If you don't have a special stone in your home, keep your eyes open for one that appeals to you. Find a spot where you can see it as you are reading this book.

Just as clay is characterized by its stony source, we, too, begin with basic body elements—the bone and flesh we are born with. Genome tracking and DNA coding remind us that nature provides a set of "givens" to work with. Bones are long or short, weak or strong. Muscles, pliable or tight. Sinews, tendons, organs, senses— all provide the basics we are born with. What is "normal"? What is not? What needs correcting? What cannot be corrected? Each body is some unique combination of strengths and weaknesses when we start. We cannot escape the nature of our bodies (although advertising would have us think that we can!).

Even though most of us identify strongly with our minds, we cannot exist without our bodies. Because form and substance join in our bodies, it is there that soulwork must begin. Paul Tillich used the term *ground of being* to distinguish this basic strata of self, of aliveness at its source. Similarly, I use the term *grounding* to describe being at home in our bodies, at ease with the natural world and particularly with the earthiness and messiness of clay.

The Nature of Your Body

- Find a picture of yourself at about eighteen months of age. Take a close look at what your body was like then. Then look for a picture of yourself at roughly three years of age, and another at six. Take special note of any changes in the way you held yourself.

- What can you see in these photographs about the "givens" of your body-self?

- How have the "givens" of your body shaped your life in adulthood?

Grounding in the physical body happens naturally at first, without thought or effort. Babies begin to explore the world through touch and taste. We know that exploration and curiosity are signs of health in a toddler. Brain studies show that direct sensate experience helps with brain development and later social capacities. While we give lip service to freedom and independence for children in our culture, we actually encourage children to separate mind and body by putting them in front of a TV screen at an early age. They are taught to take their cues from what they *see* rather than from the direct experience of what they *taste*, *touch*, and *feel*.

When children start school, they usually sit still for long periods, learning to dissociate body and mind even further. Remembering my own days in school, we daydreamed, fantasized, remembered, anticipated, and imagined all sorts of things, but in the process we learned *not* to be where we were. And with mobile technology, our culture rewards this ability to identify with our minds and basically ignore our bodies—until "they" get sick and demand attention. Urban environments also encourage this body/mind split because they cut us off from nature. Even though maintaining a healthy body has become something of an obsession in our culture, the body/mind split remains. We treat our bodies as objects to be shaped, trained, then cared for passively in old age.

But we are meant to be whole persons, grounded in our bodies and alive to the multiple currents of feeling, sensation, intuition, longings, and quirky characteristics that make us who we are. A healthy person has to find ways to be grounded in her body. A loving person has to trust the cues that his body picks up. If we are to love this world, this life, then we must be "at home" in our bodies, accepting of our mortal limits. We are indeed "dust of the earth" and "to dust we shall return." Clay can help us.

For starters, when we work with clay, we get our hands dirty. We reconnect with the mud-loving child, the natural artist, the gleeful experiencer. Although some people have a hard time entering that gate of experience because they have been taught to stay clean and neat, to avoid the elements, and to stay away from sensual exploration, I have found that recognizing the need for reconnection *as a sacred act* can make it possible to move beyond the cautions that isolate us from nature.

The very substance of clay can help us reconnect with our bodies, and with the body of earth, the Great Mother of ancient myth. Touch and physical sensation can evoke the primal matrix of creation, offering us another chance to be at home here, now.

Come with me to hunt for clay along the shore:

> *Blue silt squishes between my toes, coating my feet as earthy smells surround me walking on this winter beach. The clay holds my footprint, cupping water, then sand, from overlapping waves. My feet have found what I came for: a vein of clay, tipped and held, compressed for aeons, now exposed by a creek running into Puget Sound. I stop to dig, noting how far I will have to carry the gunnysack back to my car. The clay body is heavy and dense with seawater, but smooth as skin. I dig carefully, avoiding shells and stones. The texture is slick, full of rich nutrients. I bow to our common source, made long before I was alive.*

The Nature of Clay

- The next time you are walking outside, look for clay in your neighborhood ... in a puddle, in your garden, at an excavation site. You can spot clay by the way it cracks into little hard scales when dry or by the way it holds water when wet.

- Squeeze it tight and notice the texture. Then let it air-dry. If it holds together, it's clay. You've made a sculpture!

WATER

In the cosmic story of creation, water developed after the earth's crust cooled to stone. Even today, scientists can't tell us definitively where water first came from. Was it a random combination of hydrogen and oxygen? Some say water arrived from outer space as meteors made of ice. Others posit the natural process of chemical combination. However it happened, we know that water is essential for life—and for clay.

As the earth's creation story continued, water vapor surrounded the earth, held close by gravity, shielding the earth from the naked rays of the sun. The atmosphere was born. Soon wind and weather began their cunning work of erosion, so layers of fine stone began to wash downhill, tumbling into smaller and smaller particles. The difference between powdered stone and clay is primarily the presence of water.

Moving water and still water have different functions in making clay from stone. Rushing water grinds and tumbles stone, while pooled water allows collection, expansion, and internal change. Streams and rivers make a natural sluice, catching the heavier particles of stone in baffles of experience, while carrying lighter layers farther on, sifting and sorting in the process. Finally, the molecules of stone are finely ground and free of rocks, laid down layer upon layer wherever the water pools. These secondary clays are prized for finer work.

Water is essential for physical existence. All of us begin as water-breathers in the womb and rely on water to sustain human community. No wonder scientists look for signs of water on other planets as the best indicator for other forms of life.

Exploring Wetness

- How long has it been since you walked on wet grass with bare feet? Or splashed through a puddle without shoes? Or walked in a stream, letting your toes squish in the mud? Try it! It's a great first step toward grounding yourself in nature.

- Notice what happens at the bottom of a sloping driveway after a rainstorm: how rocks and sand move differently, how fine sand or clay collects in cracks and crevices. Is there a place in your neighborhood where you see erosion on a larger scale? What does it look like?

- How much water do you drink in a day? How do you feel when you have plenty of water? Can you remember a time when you did not have enough drinking water (on a hike or due to a storm)? What happened when you finally had water again?

Just as water breaks down stone to form clay, so, too, does the network of human relationships have a watery effect on our lives—sorting and sifting, expanding our capacity for love, forgiveness, compassion, and resistance. The stony substance we are born with is, indeed, shaped by the watery realm that surrounds us. We are dependent on a flowing stream of human relationships, our family and community, to hone our rough, unpolished edges, to give us shape and form.

The family into which we are born begins the work of erosion and creation in our capacity for relationships. We learn to let our feelings out—or hold them in. We learn whether it's all right to laugh or cry, to explore—or not. We learn to trust the world—or not. We learn to rely on our feelings to create systems of justice and mercy—or we split thinking and feeling, to the detriment of society. Without our "watery feelings" of tears and laughter, the full range of human relationships does not develop.

Just as how dry or wet a piece of clay is determines how easily it can be formed, so, too, does the web of relationships that surrounds us from birth soften or harden our feeling capacity. Although we are born with a certain temperament or sensitivity, the field of relationships around us can enhance or subdue those natural proclivities.

There are times when I am stiff and dry, in need of others to soften my hard edges. There are other times when I am drowning in a sea of e-mails or emotions, sick of responding to others' needs and needing time alone. To notice where the balance is and where the boundaries are is a soulwork task. If our feeling capacity is watered by relationships, it is important to understand the relationships that formed us and to know which relationships are especially important for us now, at this stage of our lives.

The Flow of Life

- Think about how your human connections have shaped you. Did you learn to hold your feelings in? Or to follow your heart? Has your concept of truth or entitlement hardened into rigidity? How might you let those hard places soften so they can be reworked?

- What relationships "water" your life right now? Is there plenty? Or is it dry? Which relationships are particularly key to your sense of balance? You might find it helpful to draw one or more "pools" of relationship, writing in names of specific people and the qualities they bring to your life.

- What do you do regularly to water your soul? Some people need music, dancing, other people, or fun things. Others need quiet, color, or reading. What sustains you? Where has your spiritual nurture dried up? What might you need or want to add?

SLIME

Life and death are the third ingredients of clay. The essence of clay is its pliability, its ability to be shaped by hand without a hammer or chisel, and this elasticity requires billions of tiny organisms giving their lives to make a sticky, shapeable mass of wet clay. Three-quarters of all life forms are microbial, busy going about the work of living and dying, decomposing larger life forms that, in turn, support the whole great drama of life. This organic decomposition is death in the service of life, of shapeability and possibility. Without the slime of decaying organisms, ground stone and water would simply be erosion. It is the rotted organic matter that makes the clay pliable, that makes clay hold its shape.

Pliability reminds us that the great chain of being is held in every handful of clay. Clay's sticky, gummy quality can help or harm, but it is always a reminder of clay's ubiquitous presence. Every modern gardener has fought with lumps of clay that need to be broken up and enriched for good soil, and even a bag of potting soil may contain more clay than humus.

Pliability also makes clay the earth's memory, recording the imprint of seed, claw, leaf, or fingerprint for a later time. With pressure from added layers of silt, or heat from volcanic action, natural clay layers become stone again, holding fossils that mark the cycles of climate and species for millions of years. Pressure, even without heat, can turn clay into sedimentary rock.

Beyond the earth's story, clay also holds the human story. Dry clay will hold an impression without change for aeons, and in arid climates, archaeologists have found unfired artifacts dating back thousands of years. At the National Gallery of Art in Washington, D.C., there is an unfired clay death mask that dates back to the second century BCE. Although we know little of the impulse behind these death masks, we can see evidence of imagination and interpretation in these artifacts without the permanency that firing brings. Before the last Ice Age, nomads used clay to line a bark basket, making it watertight. It wasn't long before they discovered that fire would harden clay, to make it last. Art and usefulness have gone hand-in-hand through the ages.

The Miracle of Decay

- Open your refrigerator and find something that is beginning to decay. I can usually find something in the bottom of my vegetable crisper that is slippery— something that needs to go in the compost pile rather than in the salad bowl. Organic matter has a fairly short shelf life.

- Do you garden? Or keep houseplants? How do you "enhance" the soil? Whatever form of fertilizer or compost that you prefer is an example of organic decay.

- Have you ever seen a museum display of artifacts made from clay? Or natural shapes preserved in fossils? Or pictures of an ancient bowl that someone used aeons ago for a simple task? What was your response to these memories preserved in clay?

Like the organic decay that makes clay pliable, the human gift of imagination allows us to shape our experience. Imagination gives us the power to look back, to bring the past and future into the present, and to see beyond the present. Imagination also gives us the power to change, to move beyond the bonds of genetic determinism. We can reshape our experience, reimagine another future.

Early humans used clay to paint images on cave walls. Where these ancient murals were protected from the elements of wind and water, the natural colors of iron-rich mud and charcoal have lasted for thousands of years. Although we may not know the specific meanings of these cave paintings, these pictorial representations may have given the earliest humans the power to see forward.

Looking at early cave paintings, we can "feel" the power of those great animals and imagine how a hunter might face his fears beforehand in those sacred caves. Scientists now know that imagination can create a visceral response—that we can literally feel something by hearing it or seeing it with our minds. Holding a piece of clay invites movement, asks our fingers to play—to stretch, press, stroke, smooth where the clay begins to crack. Even the act of holding clay can stir a visceral response beyond thought. Something entirely new can be born in that instant— out of action, before thought. It's not that we imagine a finished product, but that we can be in conversation with the clay. We can let its nature speak to us and invite us into a new form together. If we can keep from jumping to conclusions—forcing the clay into a predetermined form—something new can be born.

Where does that newness come from? Is it possible that our human responsiveness is part of the way the universe reflects on itself? Adjusts to assaults? Adapts to new conditions? Are we one of the ways that the earth adapts to the ravages caused by our notions of progress? How do we honor the gifts of consciousness and creativity that each of us has? These questions are the essence of soulwork that clay invites us to explore.

The Gateway to Imagination

- Take a beloved object or a small piece of clay and sit quietly with it in your hand for a few minutes. Let the mud-loving child in you respond to it. Let the object or clay be your guide. Let your fingers explore. Let your feelings speak. Be especially aware of any thoughts, ideas, or feelings that come to mind.

- What activities have encouraged your imaginative life? You might want to find or create an example to share with a close friend.

- Are there things you once enjoyed, that kindled your imagination, but you are no longer doing? How might you renew that spark of imagination? Or are there new interests that are now available, or that you would like to pursue?

RITUAL, SYMBOL, AND STORY

The raw material of clay is so common that we forget how important it has been in the history of the earth and of humankind. Is that because clay is so like us? So available and lasting, even without firing? Anyone can have the experience of taking mud from the edge of a pond and making a small figure with it. No special tools are required.

Nearly every culture mentions clay in its creation myth. The biblical creation story pictures God scooping up a handful of clay, shaping a human creature, and breathing life into it. Thus, spirit enters flesh, according to that story written down on tablets of clay some five thousand years ago. The mystery of how life began is extended to include the sexual differentiation of man and woman—attraction and repulsion, the basis for love and passion and desire, as well as separateness and destruction. Feeling and imagination are included in this primal story that has so shaped our understanding of soulwork.

We are the storytellers and symbol-makers who work with clay to make things. Created with the capacity to wonder, to observe and examine the microscopic elements of life, to feel the whole in every part, and to create something new, we are instinctively drawn to clay as a natural medium for human creativity.

Because clay is a part of nature's cycle, it links us with a larger unified field of interconnection with all of life. Some of the marks and figures of early pictographs speak across the centuries of reverence and connection with all parts of the natural world. Ancient humans knew themselves to be part of a living network, an organic whole. But that connection with the unified field of life was largely unconscious. It would take the patriarchal period to achieve individual self-consciousness. Then Greek thought split body and spirit, associating *spiritus* with eternal ideals, light, air, and sky gods, which left the unconscious body as little more than a beast of burden. Religion picked up that theme by associating *logos* with reason, language, thought, purity, and, ultimately, with God as Father—which left the bloody mystery of body and birth to nature, earth, and Mother. The scientific revolution reinforced that split by associating consciousness with masculine thought and enlightenment, while feelings were associated with unconscious feminine intuition.

We are all—men and women—children of that patriarchal period of history. And it has cost us dearly. We seem to have lost our sense of connection with each other and with the earth as the unified field in which we are interdependent with all things. We operate as individual units, barely conscious of the consequences. The industrial ideal of "progress" has allowed us to do irreparable damage to the earth, water supplies, and the atmosphere we breathe, and still we plunge on, accumulating more than we need or even want.

Even our sense of what is "art" has become fragmented. Art once flowed out of the natural rhythms of life, and clay told the story of human civilization. The earliest sacred figurines were made of clay and hardened by fire. Bricks of clay and straw built pyramids and temples that are still standing after five thousand years. Fired bricks from Babylon still glow with vibrant color on the Gates of Ishtar. But today, art is the purview of specialists. Although clay has long been considered a lesser art than painting or sculpture, ceramics also straddles the realms of spirit and commerce—in danger of being captured by experts. Treasured bowls are bartered between modern museums for millions of dollars. Every day we make local decisions to remove art and music from the public school curriculum in favor of testable subjects. I believe this fragmentation is part of the reason why we humans can do so much damage to the environment without remorse: we don't carry a picture of the whole; we don't identify with creation's story as our story, too.

At its core, soulwork is about recovering that unified field of interconnection among all things. It's time to find our way back to being part of the earth's survival—and our own. I believe that something as simple as working with clay can provide that path. I'm not talking about becoming a potter, necessarily, but finding enough clay to make it part of our imaginative life. We can bring the best of our thinking skills to the intuitive field of sensate awareness and marry them together in the soulwork of clay. That will, in turn, give birth to new stories and rituals, new creativity that we need to heal the wounds that we ourselves have created so heedlessly. The capacity for recovering the sense of the whole is found in every person. This is work that everyone can do—the inner path of soulwork.

Creating a Soulwork Space

- When referring to clay, most potters will ask, "What kind of a body do you use?" They are speaking about the color and texture and firing temperature of different kinds of clay. Like our own physical bodies, the clay body provides the basic elements that we have to work with. To reflect on your "basic elements," select one of the pictures of yourself that you used for "The Nature of Your Body" exercise. Take special notice of your body, the expression on your face, and who else is in the picture with you.

- Put the picture, together with a special stone, in a place where you will be aware of them at the beginning and end of each day for a week or so. You might place them on a small cloth, just to set the space apart as a sacred spot for contemplation. Then, when you are ready, spend some time exploring these questions (you might want to keep a journal of your responses):

  ◆ What kind of a body were you born with?

  ◆ Where did your name come from?

  ◆ What stories do you recall of your first year? What do you know about the circumstances of your family then?

  ◆ What does your special stone suggest to you?

- You may want to add some other stones and some other pictures to your sacred space. If the picture you selected is yourself at a very young age, you might add some pictures of yourself at several older ages. Notice any changes in your body or the way you held yourself in front of the camera.

  ◆ Were you shy or bold? Aware or unconscious of the camera?

  ◆ Was the picture taken indoors or out?

  ◆ What do you know about where and how you spent time outdoors, in nature? Did you have any experience with clay or mud as a youngster?

◆ What were your favorite stories as a child? Did you have any bedtime rituals that helped you rest easy in the "unified field" of sleep?

COMING HOME TO CLAY

Given my belief that clay can help us recover our sense of connection with the very ground we walk on, it is ironic that my years as a professional potter actually *separated* me from the wonder and mystery of clay because I was so caught up in practical matters of production and sales. But, after many years of focus on glazing and decoration, I have come home to the clay body again. This new form of my journey with clay happened by "accident."

I was on my way to lead a retreat when I got a phone call saying that our friend Michael Vermillion had been in a terrible auto accident. When I got to the hospital, his brother informed me that Michael was brain dead and that the family had decided to take him off the ventilator. He would die soon. His brother asked, "Could you make a container for Michael's ashes so we can scatter them over his crab pots in the Chesapeake Bay?"

"I do have clay in the car," I said, "but I don't have time to fire a pot."

"Perfect," he replied, "the clay will dissolve with the ashes."

And so I sat, on a steamy August day, pinching a large vessel to hold the remains of my dear friend, someone who had believed in me and my call to a nontraditional form of ministry. As an ordained priest, Michael had cheered me on beyond the boundaries of religious denominations ... but now he was gone.

It wasn't until nearly a decade later that the call to make unfired burial urns came again. This time it was from a young couple in our church. They had been searching for an appropriate place to bury the remains of their child who had died at birth, and they decided to scatter her ashes in the Lake of the Saints at Dayspring, the

Church of the Saviour retreat center of which our community, Seekers Church, is a part owner.

Could I, along with the children of our community (including their two daughters), make a container for her ashes? I was honored to be asked and brought clay to the next family retreat at Dayspring. Seven or eight children gathered round to ask their questions and press their fingers into the clay as we made the urn together. After a simple ceremony to pour the ashes into the still-damp clay vessel, the children covered the top with daisies, and we paraded down the hill toward the lake in solemn procession. The urn sank, to dissolve with its precious cargo, and the daisies floated away slowly in the setting sun. It was a tender, beautiful time that allowed all of us to participate. We had made it holy with our hearts wide open.

Unfired burial urn
by Marjory Zoet Bankson.

Since then, I have made many urns designed for impermanence, chalices to carry someone's ashes to his or her final resting place. Each urn is different, unique, and special, like the person whose remains it will hold. Some are thrown on a wheel, and others are hand-built. Because these pots are meant to return to the earth, I feel a great freedom about surface decoration. Literally, these raw clay containers cradle ashes making the transit "from dust to dust."

A year after we buried my mother's ashes in one of these unfired burial urns, I had a dream that seemed to bless my impulse to move in this new direction with clay:

> *I am in a spare mountain cabin at night. My mother is lying peacefully in a double bed beneath a lovely quilt. I know she is dying. I ask her if she'd like to go outside and see the full moon. She nods, and I pick her up in my arms, wrapped in the quilt.*

17

*She's heavier than I thought, and I lean against the doorjamb.
"Would you scoot the rocker over?" I ask my sister, who
seems to be outside in the dark. I hear the rocking chair move
in behind me. I sit down with my mother on my lap, looking
out at the full moon over the shadowy trees and ridgeline. I
tuck the quilt around us both and feel at peace.*

Later, when I drew this dream in my journal, I saw the doorway as a
passageway from death and separation to a unified field of moon,
mother, and ongoing life. It felt like a blessing from beyond for the
work I was about to engage in: writing this book about the soulwork
of clay.

In the opening chapter of *Centering: In Poetry, Pottery, and the
Person*, M. C. Richards tells an ancient Chinese story about a potter. A nobleman riding through town sees a humble peasant potter
at work and stops to admire the pots. When he asks the potter how
he is able to make vessels that "possess such convincing beauty," the
potter replies, "You are looking at the mere outward shape. What I
am forming lies within."

This takes us to the core of soulwork, the process of connecting
the inward and outward dimensions of our lives. If we are going to
recover our capacity for love and wonder, if we are going to restore
our sense of community with each other and all creation, if we are
going to love the earth enough to save it from destruction, then the
school for our souls can be as close as clay.

Try It with Clay!

FINDING CLAY

The easiest source of clay is your local craft supplier. Look in the yellow pages under "craft instruction and supplies." Not all craft stores have clay, so be sure to check first. A small package of self-hardening clay will be fine for your first experiment, although you may want a larger amount of regular clay that could be fired later, if you intend to try all of the exercises in this book. Potters generally buy clay in 25-pound bags, which come two to a box from a clay supplier. Once opened, those bags must be kept tightly closed between uses or the clay will dry out. Although clay can be softened again with water, it's a chore.

DIGGING CLAY

You may also have a natural source of clay nearby. If you live in an area where the older houses are made of bricks, you probably live where clay is easy to find. Often there are layers of clay along a stream or road cut, which you can recognize by the smooth, slippery, compact texture and the way it weathers, with deep eroded gullies.

Because wet clay will hold water, you can sometimes locate a natural vein of clay that way. If there is clay in a mud puddle, the surface will look cracked and scaly when it dries up. You can collect that dry clay in a plastic bag and add a little water to test whether the clay will hold together. It should become a sticky mass that will hold a shape.

Wet clay usually needs to be dried and pulverized, sifted to remove rocks and sticks, and then mixed with water. In the Southwest there are known sources of clay that come out of the

Unglazed bowl with incised decoration by Louie Mideke.

ground dry and pebbly, ready to be sifted on site. The sifting breaks the clay into a cornmeal-like consistency. Then it is mixed with volcanic ash to help the clay withstand the thermal shock of open-pit firing, and it can be used almost immediately.

This small unglazed bowl was one that my pottery teacher, Louie Mideke, made of local Bellingham, Washington, clay. No additives were needed. The pattern was incised directly into the clay body, then fired to cone 8 in a gas kiln (I'll explain more about firing in chapter 7).

Every potter tests her clay for elasticity because it is such an important quality for hand-building or throwing on a potter's wheel. Some clay is "short," denied the glue of slippery decay, forever breaking into sandy bits instead of clinging to the shape that fingers make. By contrast, other clay has too much ooze and will not hold an upright shape.

If you want to test an unknown source of clay, the process is relatively simple. Children typically "make a snake" with clay when they first get it, and that's a good test for pliability. Roll the clay between your fingertips and see whether you can make a rope of clay that will hold together enough to make a circle about the size of a silver dollar. If you can, the clay is pliable enough to use. If it cracks when curled into a circle, then the clay is too "short" and will need to be mixed with a more plastic clay. Ball clay or EPK (Edgar Plastic Kaolin) can be purchased for that purpose.

FINGER-PRESSED PATTERNS

When wet, clay is pliable and will record an impression made by your fingers or a tool. When the clay dries, that impression will last. Although ancient people used clay to line baskets and make them watertight, they soon recognized that clay could be decorated simply by pressing it with their fingers. You have probably seen people decorate the edge of a pie this way, by squeezing it into a crimped edge with their fingers.

Roll out a rope of clay and try some different patterns of crimping until you find one that you like—and keep it as a texture you might try on the rim of a vessel later on.

The wonderful thing about clay is that nothing is wasted. What you don't like, you can just wad up and use again. If the clay begins to get dry, put it in a plastic bag and spritz it with water. In a day or two, the dry clay will have absorbed the water, and you can use it again.

STEPPINGSTONES

Along with the natural stone(s) in your "soulwork space," you might try adding a handmade "stone" or flat-textured button for each picture you have displayed there.

Begin with a small piece of clay and pat it into a "steppingstone." You could add a "baby footprint," which can be made by pressing the pinkie-finger side of your closed hand into the clay and then using your index finger to make the toe imprints.

Sit quietly, focusing on each picture until you can identify a feeling that you have about the body and soul of that child—yourself at a much younger age. Think about how you might want to decorate the steppingstone or button for each picture to reflect that feeling.

Pressed patterns, burnished and sawdust fired.

Then go to your kitchen to find something with which you can add texture—the edge of a spoon, a sponge, a string, a toothpick, a key. Once you start thinking in terms of texture rather than object, your kitchen contains an infinite number of tools for texturing. These steppingstones might give you a few ideas. (These buttons have been fired in sawdust, which I'll explain in chapter 7.)

Once your steppingstones or buttons are dry, you can color them by scrubbing pastel chalk on a piece of paper to create some chalk dust, then picking up the color on your fingers and simply rubbing the raw textured clay to create a soft color that will emphasize the texture.

Variation: Beads

You can also make clay beads by sliding a small-gauge knitting needle through a small ball of clay and then tapping it firmly on a texture. I have used intricately carved woodblocks from other countries, small cookie molds, and jewelry to make bead patterns. If you later fire these beads and string them, you'll need to determine which size knitting needle to use to allow for shrinkage of the clay and "fit" for your stringing material (leather, woven cord, embroidery floss).

Clay bead pattern.

These clay "stones" can easily turn into little fish, with a few pinches for the tail and fins. Play with the clay and see whether you can create a fish that makes you smile.

BURNISHING

Another method for finishing your "stone" (or any clay piece) is a very ancient technique of creating a gloss on the surface of clay by burnishing it with a smooth pebble or a spoon. Using the back curved surface of the spoon, rub a small area of the clay with a circular motion to a fine sheen. What you are doing is compacting the molecules of the clay. This will not make your piece any more permanent, but it will give it a lovely natural luster. Using the back of a silver spoon will usually add a slightly gray sheen to white clay.

The pot pictured at right is made of unfired porcelain clay, burnished slightly to show the texture of the surface and colored inside with pastel chalk. Traditional artisans burnish a piece while it is still damp (leather-hard) and then create a pattern by cutting or scratching through the burnish to create a dull line in a shiny surface. You may want to try that, too.

Unfired burnished clay with chalk-colored interior.

Terra Sigillata

Burnishing is improved by the application of *terra sigillata*, a watery slurry of clay that can be brushed onto the dried surface of any clay piece, then rubbed gently with the palm of your hand or a soft flannel cloth to give it a polish. The bowl pictured at right has been covered with *terra sigillata*, burnished with a flannel cloth, and fired in a charcoal grill (which I'll describe in chapter 7).

Pinched bowl brushed with *terra sigillata*, burnished and sawdust fired.

To make your own *terra sigillata*, here is a recipe that I have used with good results:

> **400 grams** dry clay (ball clay or any other finely ground surface clay)
>
> **4 grams** soda ash or 2 teaspoons water softener (such as Calgon)
>
> **1 quart** warm water

Combine the dry clay and soda ash or water softener in a bowl. Sift the clay/ash mixture onto the water and let the water absorb it. Shake well or blend for 5 minutes in a blender and pour through a very fine (100 mesh) screen. Let the mixture settle overnight. The slip will be

Small burnished pot from the Santa Clara Pueblo in New Mexico.

thin, like muddy water. If the slip is really good, there will be very little clear water on top. Siphon off the *top half* of the muddy water—this is your *terra sigillata.* (Do NOT try to pour the *terra sigillata* off because you will get heavier particles from the bottom half of the mixture. You can use a turkey baster to suck off the top half of the liquid if you are very careful. For a large batch, purchase a gasoline siphon with a hand pump.) Throw away the bottom half of the mixture.

If you have seen the stunning black pots made by Maria Martinez and other pueblo potters from the American Southwest, you have seen this method of burnishing developed to a fine art. She uses a fine slip of watery clay over her pots, burnishes them with a smooth stone, then paints or carves a matte pattern over the burnished surface. The striking black color is achieved by firing in a smoky environment (see chapter 7 for more about firing). The pot pictured above came from the Santa Clara pueblo and is an example of a burnished surface with slip decoration.

2

Kneading

Preparation and Readiness

On my knees, I press the clay down onto a board,
then lift and turn slightly, then press again,
to mix all parts together.

Before the day's work begins, most people go through some preparation rituals: stretching, bathing, dressing, eating, drinking coffee, finding car keys, and such. The routine marks the transition between sleeping and waking, between the metaphysical realm of dream images, and the linear path of rational thought. It is a borderland, a threshold on which to pause and gather ourselves for the work ahead.

Kneading clay is a preparation ritual. Clay and potter are becoming acquainted, measuring strength, and loosening tight places so that the dance of life can proceed with full participation. The rhythmic motion of kneading is designed to mix soft and hard parts of the clay into a uniform mass. Anyone who has made bread or watched a baker prepare her dough will know the motion: pressing downward with the heels of your hands and then lifting and twisting slightly with your fingertips so that air is not trapped in a pocket. Such air pockets contain moisture that would expand when heated. In clay, trapped moisture can burst during the firing. Careful kneading is the best way to prevent that.

When I am kneading, my whole body is involved, as in a yoga or tai chi exercise. I feel as though I am bowing to the clay. It requires no particular thought, but it serves to awaken my intuition and imagination. It is a body-prayer between what I can clutch and count, and the inner realm of intuition and inspiration. Kneading is an invitation to focus, to be conscious of the present moment with my whole being.

AWAKENING

Typically, I knead all of the clay that I will be using in a day as part of my morning ritual of readiness. Using a large plywood board, I kneel at one edge, using my body weight to keep the board from moving as I rock forward, pressing the heels of my hands along one edge in order to press the clay out against the board. Rocking back, my fingertips guide the clay up and around into position to press it down again, just to one side of the first pressing. After five or six pressings, I can see the twisted swirl that my hands are creating. The spiral, like the whorl of a conch shell, indicates that I am kneading the clay effectively, not trapping air in the overlap between each press.

Kneading clay.

Not only do I lean my weight against the clay, but the clay also has its own way of pressing back, resisting my action, reminding me that the clay has its own substance and character. As my body speaks and the clay answers back with its texture and toughness, I begin to imagine what I might do with that batch of clay. I get to know who it is and what it can do. The clay and I begin a dialogue, there on the floor, grunting and pushing in the morning stillness.

In the beginning, I did not recognize that kneading was actually the first stage of making a pot. I thought of kneading as something to get through, to finish quickly, so I could get to the *real* work. I gave it just enough attention to do the job right—make sure there were no air bubbles, make sure the whole mass got mixed and not just the softer parts—but no more. Without thinking, I would turn on the radio and let sound distract me from this preparation phase. Eventually, my body complained about this lack of attention. I developed a wrist pain that was nagging and sharp even before I got to the potter's wheel. I realized I was doing something wrong in the kneading process, hurting myself in some way. I tried various ways to change my position, but nothing seemed to work—until I noticed the music that was always playing in the background.

To listen to my body more carefully, I turned off the radio and listened in the silence. It didn't take long to feel the adjustment that I needed to make, but by then I realized something more: that kneading was an important time to gather myself, to bring my conscious attention to the clay and the creative process we were engaged in. My body—shoulders, arms, wrists, and hands—was full of guidance about the way to be in relationship with the clay, but I had been too distracted to hear. Now I purposely do most of my creative work in silence, so I can listen more attentively to my body speech.

I had assumed that my body was unconscious, incapable of speech. I had been living into the separation of body and spirit, unaware that soulwork demands body involvement. Pain gave me a way into this mysterious reality of body speech and body connection. I began to treat kneading as a form of body-prayer, awakening to the recognition that I was part of something more fundamental. Now I call that the presence of God or the universal Source.

The motions of kneading take me back to early childhood and link my body with countless generations of humans learning to crawl, stand, and, finally, walk and speak. Infants are not simply built to move; their early movement experiences are essential for brain development. Rocking on hands and knees is thought to stimulate the parts of the brain needed for internal organization of thought and speech. It's especially interesting that new brain research is showing that movement, because it activates our neural wiring, makes *the entire body*, not just the brain, an instrument of learning!

Have you ever heard of "neurobic" exercise? Lawrence Katz, a professor of neurobiology at Duke University Medical Center, has created a system of brain exercises that puts the five senses to work in unexpected ways, such as intentionally pairing two senses together to activate underused nerve pathways. I have to smile: one of his suggested exercises is to "watch the clouds and play with clay at the same time." I don't think this is incidental. Engaging in the physicality of clay, with the accompanying sensual sights, sounds, and smells, awakens us to more than the possibilities of clay. We come alive to *our* possibilities as well.

If we have lived mostly in our heads, the physical motions of rocking, pressing, and turning to form a spiral in the clay can awaken our whole bodies for the living of each day. When I am kneading clay, I am reconnecting with the primary center of self through my body motions. The clay teaches me to be present and fully awake in the moment, to *be* in the doing. Kneading becomes a ritual of gathering the disparate parts of myself—plans, interruptions, dreams, stray bits of conversation, song—and bringing everything to a single point of concentration as I move to the second and third batch of clay with my prayer-full routine. I am fully present, listening, ready.

Awakening can happen at any stage in life. In the last week of my mother's life, she had a remarkable dream of crawling on her hands and knees that reminded me of the motions involved in kneading:

> *I've been chosen to go with a group of women through the veil of mystery. We're crawling, single file, along a wooden plank or walkway, hunting for the opening.*

After she told me the dream, she said quietly, "I guess I'm crawling now." She said that she didn't know the other women in the line, but she knew they had all been called to go. She was curious about the veil of mystery but didn't need to know more.

The next few days were amazing. She said her "thank-yous" and "good-byes" to all who came ... and there were many. She said that made her feel humble, and I could see that it did. She kept saying, "I'm on my hands and knees and it doesn't hurt. It doesn't hurt."

I believe that the dream gave her the courage to choose hospice care rather than radical intervention for congestive heart failure. At the age of ninety-one, she had lived a full life and was ready to go; the dream seemed to reassure her that there was something beyond this life, although it was hidden beyond "the veil of mystery."

When her breathing became more difficult, we talked about death as another kind of birth experience that would be hard and intense, but not too long. The image of crawling on her hands and knees seemed to help her take that in. She was ready, willing to let go of her body and shake loose of its pain. She was awakening to another reality in those last days of her life.

Rituals of Readiness

- How do you gather yourself for the work of each day? What are the rituals of readiness that you perform? Things like showering, shaving, dressing, eating, even driving, can be done as a prayer practice if you are conscious of them in that way. Is there one practice you might focus on with more awareness?

- When you begin to work with clay, getting to know the clay will help awaken you to what you might do with it. If you have a piece of clay, pinch off five equal pieces and roll them into balls. Look at them closely to see whether they are of the same size. Pick up each piece individually and see whether you can feel any weight differences. The more you practice this, the more you can grow in your sensitivity to the clay's weight and mass.

BREATHING

Kneading posture requires a deeper kind of breathing. Shallow breathing from the upper chest is not enough. As I rock forward, the motion forces the old air out of my lower lungs, and my whole body fills naturally as I rock back on my heels. The motion is a meditation practice: eyes open, breathing synchronized and deep. It fills me with air and releases tension, bringing all of me to relaxed attentiveness. I suspect that my rhythm of kneading and breathing happens in tune with my heartbeat.

When I first began conscious kneading, I realized that I did not know how to breathe fully. I became aware of chronic tightness in my chest and throat, as though I were holding my voice in readiness for a critical question. But kneading cannot be sustained with such constriction. I had to find a way to relax and still apply pressure, the way a skater or a dancer does.

Eastern mystics know that the breath is a pathway to all that is holy, but we Westerners talk more about lung capacity and endurance than awareness through breathing. Later, when I learned about centering prayer, I realized that kneading had already opened that door, taught me to rest in the rhythm of my breath, and given me some experience in moving beyond the "squirrel cage" of worries, plans, and egoic thought. My body was teaching me about prayer at the primal level of bone and blood, lungs and air.

Most of our breathing is performed unconsciously, but it is interesting to note that breathing is one of the few bodily functions that can be performed *both* unconsciously and consciously. During sleep, for example, we usually breathe deeply and fully, oblivious to the in-and-out movement of our breath. But to discover ways of staying *conscious* and breathing fully, with the whole body, is another practice entirely.

Conscious breathing as a spiritual practice has been embraced by many of our spiritual ancestors, from the Christian Desert Fathers and Mothers, to Hindu Yogis, Islamic Sufis, and the Buddha. Conscious breathing is exactly how it sounds: being fully aware of every breath, as you inhale and exhale. It is a way of being fully present, unified in body, mind, and spirit. It is a way to mend the fragmentation that we create with our minds, the suffering and worry that come from imagining dire results in the future or retelling the stories of hurt from the past. As a spiritual practice, conscious breathing brings us fully into the present moment, into the reality of now.

There have been times of trauma in my life when I have gone to my studio and simply kneaded clay because it was deeply grounding, deeply peaceful. The gentle rocking motion felt comforting, perhaps even recalling the safety and security of the womb. I had learned that this kneading-prayer would get me beyond my fears. Once I was mugged by two teenage boys while walking home from the grocery store. Although I cried out, nobody heard me or came to my rescue. They ran off with my purse and everything that was in it, including my house keys. Fortunately, I was not far from home, and the house was open. After cruising the neighborhood with a policeman, I went back home and locked the doors. Then I went to my studio and spent an hour or so kneading clay, mindlessly rocked and comforted by that motion. I told myself that it was to prepare for the next day, but now I know that I was trying to move beyond fear. I was both soothing my injured body and remembering my place in a greater story—that what I had suffered was neither more nor less important than what millions of others face every day. Kneading reminded me not only that I was safe and grounded in my own home, but also that I was loved and cared for by unseen hands. When I was finished, and had a nice pile of kneaded clay to work with, I slept peacefully. Like my mother's dream of crawling toward the veil of mystery, the practice of kneading had called my soul to rest.

The Breath of Life

- Take a few minutes to focus on your breathing. Let your belly relax and fill with air like a balloon. Pause a moment to be conscious of the feeling, and then release all the air, squeezing slightly with your stomach muscles at the end of each full breath. Don't force it. Let the rest of your body relax. Notice how your whole body feels at the end of this time.

- Take one of the small balls of clay that you created in the "Rituals of Readiness" exercise and hold it in the palm of one hand. With the thumb of your other hand, open the clay at the center, pressing down to about ½ from the bottom. Then, with your thumb on the inside and forefinger on the outside, pinch a small "doughnut" of clay around the hole. Then begin to pinch a small bowl by repeating this motion in a slow spiral from the base to the rim. Do your pinching in rhythm with your slow, relaxed breathing. Pinch as you exhale, then rotate the clay as you inhale. Continue with this slow breathing-and-pinching motion to discover what the clay can do. If you notice your mind wandering from the point of contact between your fingers and the clay, just stop. And breathe. And begin pinching again.

LISTENING

The practice of kneading in silence helped me learn to listen for inner sounds. When I turned off the radio, even without knowing that I was listening for something deeper, I began to notice the inner voices that had been disguised by the background music. Some were encouraging, and others were critical. Often I would begin the day with eagerness and expectation, and the motion of kneading massaged a magical womb of images and ideas that seemed to be waiting to be birthed into form. I could hear joy in my body at a deep, internal level of spiritual creativity. It was my soul, longing for life.

At other times, my mind was blank. Nothing appeared. Then an accusing voice would begin: "See? You can't do this. Potting is a waste of time. And money. You'll never be good enough to make a living like this! What about your fancy education? What are you doing with that?" I learned to listen for those inner harpies and follow the sound back to some event that needed attention. But I discovered another voice, too. Quieter. Closer to my heart. Seemingly tidal, it was the pulsing wave of possibility. I began to call that voice "the Encourager," from the French word for heart, *le coeur*.

"Have courage," she seemed to say, "take heart." In the silence, the Encourager whispered, "Be a beginner. Give yourself time. Let your hands learn. Your body knows the way. Relax. Listen. Practice."

Inner Messages

- Take a few minutes to jot down inner messages that you are aware of ... and what prompts them. You might write these on Post-It notes, so you can group them at a later time and give each group a name (such as "gentle," "critical," "coach").

- Notice which voices you would like to encourage, and which you'd like to mute more.

Being conscious of those inner messages gave me more choices about how to respond. I began to move away from the shrill critics that I carried from years of academic striving. I began letting my breath take me deeper into a dialogue with the clay, allowing myself to be a learner, and thus a beginner, again and again. In the daily quiet of my pottery studio, I began to trust the Encourager. Mistakes mattered less and less. I could always rework the clay and start again. To punish myself for not already knowing how to make a particular shape was to short-circuit the process of learning.

Professional potters generally reprocess used clay with a pug mill, which is a very useful piece of machinery if you are working with large amounts of used clay. In Japan, there is usually an apprentice or a worker whose sole job is to reprocess clay for a whole studio of potters. But for me, the process of reclaiming clay from the slop bucket became more than a utilitarian chore. Deciding to consign a pot to the slop bucket was an invitation to another kind of truth— that nothing is wasted and everything can be redeemed. Every mistake became a chance to learn, if I gave my attention to it. Dry clay can always be pulverized and slaked with water until it is soft and workable again.

Over time, I began to understand that kind of kneading— reworking the clay that I had used and spoiled on the wheel—as redemptive, a chance to love my mistakes into newness. It was a commitment to process rather than product. I began to understand forgiveness as the process of letting go of one thing in order to focus on another. Gradually, I realized that kneading was not simply a task I had to do before the real work of potting could begin. Instead, kneading was a center point, the ritual of bringing myself to the clay as a pilgrim and a seeker, ready to listen for a deeper kind of guidance than I had been aware of before.

Listening for that inner voice of wisdom, and trusting it, is now at the core of my spiritual journey. Kneading awakened her voice, gave it time and space each day. That, in turn, helped ground me in my body and trust it for timing and discernment. Kneading has also opened the way for me to pay attention to my dream images. I began to perceive them as a way of "kneading" experiences from the day-world, reworking them so I could see them from a larger perspective. I began reading C. G. Jung on the importance of dreams, and started tracking my dreams in ways suggested by Jungian analyst James Hillman in *The Dream and the Underworld*. I began to understand that my unconscious flesh is longing for voice, for consciousness, so I can deal with the questions of my life—with all the awareness of a baby and the cumulative experience of my adult years.

Contemplative Review

- When do you reprocess the events of your day? How do you do that? Do you work with your dreams? Belong to a group of some sort where you can share your inner voices? Have a therapist or spiritual director? Most of us cannot do this work of awakening and listening alone, so it is helpful to consider who you can reclaim the "mistakes" of the day with.

- Forgiveness can also be an experience of reworking events over time, softening the hard edges of resentment with greater understanding or tenderness. Can you think of an example from your own life?

- Take the small bowl you pinched in "The Breath of Life" exercise and sit quietly with it. Imagine that it is filled with something you regret. Stay present to that experience as fully as you can, and then, without anger or despair, simply destroy the piece with your hand. Then make a new shape with the clay. (If the clay is dry, you will need to put it in a plastic bag, spritz it with water, and knead it in the bag until the clay is moist again.)

We live in a world of distractions, of instant messaging and constant connection. Kneading clay can teach us the value of solitary silence, of retreat and reflection as an integral part of soulmaking. Kneading is not a return to blissful unconsciousness, but an active way to awaken and listen for the wisdom of our bodies, the *knowing* we too often ignore. The more I pay attention to body-prayers of rocking back and forth on the floor, pressing the clay in a long spiral, the more the images of my body's wisdom are released—and the more sure I am about living consciously into the future with my whole body, not just my mental pictures.

Kneading is a daily reminder of our soul's journey through time. The motion of kneading clay by hand is a marvelous exercise in humility (from the same root as *humus*, *humanity*, and *humanness*), in knowing and loving our imperfections, in accepting our mistakes and our fumbling beginning efforts. Kneading tells us that nothing is permanent, everything will change over time, and all parts of our lives can be remixed and used again. Conscious breathing combined with conscious kneading becomes a body-prayer that invites our whole selves into the process.

Try It with Clay!

BASIC KNEADING

If you are using commercially prepared clay, it has already been screened and thoroughly mixed, but it has probably been standing on a shelf long enough that the water in the clay has migrated toward the bottom of the plastic bag that is keeping it moist. Even if you are using a small amount, the clay will need to be mixed by hand. If your piece is about the size of a small orange, the simplest way to knead it is to simply work the clay into a ball by rolling it on a tabletop.

For a larger piece, you can practice kneading it on a wooden board or tabletop—just as you would with bread dough. Press the clay down and away from you on a hard surface, and then turn it slightly as you lift it toward yourself with your fingertips before doing that again. You should begin to see a spiral pattern developing on one side of the mass or the other. That will show you that you are not trapping air by folding the flattened mass directly toward yourself. It takes a little practice to knead the clay in a spiral, but I have found this method to be a very satisfying prayer practice that combines concentration and rhythmic movement.

Another method of kneading is to cut the clay into two pieces, then turn one of those pieces (so the two cut sides don't simply rejoin) before slapping the two pieces together forcefully. By repeating that action again and again, you will gradually mix the clay thoroughly. This is especially useful if some of the clay is too hard to knead easily (which may be the case if it's been sitting in the bag so long that some of the clay is pretty dry).

USING A KNEADING BOARD

A working studio will probably have a kneading board, which is a canvas-covered plaster bat with a cutting wire that is permanently strung on a diagonal for easy use. The block of plaster is useful for absorbing excess moisture from clay that has been reprocessed by soaking in water. The canvas covering prevents flecks of plaster from being picked up during the kneading process. (Those flecks of plaster hold moisture that will expand or explode when the clay is fired.)

If you are reprocessing clay on such a kneading board, a permanently installed cutting wire speeds the process because you can cut a dryish lump of clay apart, dip both pieces into water, and rejoin them by kneading the water into the clay on the kneading board.

MAKING A CUTTING WIRE

If you are working alone and do not have access to a kneading board with a cutting wire, it is easy to make a cutting wire with fine-gauge monofilament (fishing line) and a clothespin to hold one end of it.

Using a heavy gauge of monofilament fishing line, cut about 30 inches of line and double it over for a 15-inch cutting wire.

Run the mid-loop through the metal spring of a wooden clothespin and thread the two equal lengths through the loop to secure it to the clothespin.

Holding onto one length, twist the other length tightly. Then hold that twisted length securely to keep it from unwinding while you twist the other length *in the same direction.*

Now you are ready to let the two lengths of fishing line twist themselves together. Hold the two raw ends and release the clothespin, so the two strands twist together. Tie a knot to join the two raw ends. *Note:* If one strand has not been twisted as much as the other, you can repeat these steps before knotting the completed cutting wire.

It's always tempting just to use a piece of monofilament to cut through clay, but there are two pitfalls that can be avoided by twisting the fishing line as I've described above. One is that the fishing line is nearly invisible and can easily get scooped up with scraps of clay and remixed—with disastrous results for a later piece. The other is that the slight serration caused by the twisted line helps separate one piece of moist clay from the other by making space for minute bits of air at each juncture.

COIL BUILDING

Before the use of a potter's wheel was common, many cultures created all of their functional bowls by building up the shape with coils of clay and then smoothing the coils with a gourd scraper so the ropes of clay completely disappear. Those traditional methods are still used where cultural patterns are deeply embedded in the social structure. For us, where round forms can be made quickly and easily on a wheel, coiling has become more of an art form for creating asymmetrical or irregular shapes.

Sometimes, however, clay is not pliable enough to throw on a wheel or withstand the heat-shock of a direct flame during firing. In New Mexico, for example, there are seams of natural clay that are so full of mica (a tempering agent) that pots can be used for cooking over an open flame without adding anything else to the clay during the kneading process—but the clay is not pliable enough to hold its shape on a wheel. In other parts of the world, potters have learned to add a tempering agent such as sand or pulverized fired clay during the kneading process in order to space out the clay molecules and reduce shrinkage during firing. (Anyone who has worked with grout in setting tiles around a sink or bathtub will know the usefulness of adding sand to counteract shrinkage.) If you have purchased clay from a supplier, however, the clay is probably ready for

2-1

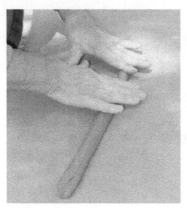

2-2

2-3

coiling without adding anything but your own sweet energy through the kneading process.

Kneading is especially important for coil building without a wheel because the coils must be uniform in thickness and texture in order to hold together. To begin this exercise, weigh out a 3-pound piece of clay and knead it thoroughly so that all the parts for your coil bowl will be made from a uniform mass of clay.

Begin by patting out a pancake of clay between your palms, and then lay it on a paper towel in a shallow bowl (a small wooden salad bowl will work well for this) [2-1]. The bowl is your *puki* (supporting dish), which can be turned as you would a wheel.

Now roll out a coil of clay about ½ inch thick, using your fingertips and not the palms of your hands. As the coil lengthens, your fingertips will naturally spread to lengthen the coil [2-2]. It's not as easy as it sounds to do this without breaking the coil. Practice until you get the feel of your clay, and work on one coil at a time, so your coils don't dry out too much. Each coil should be long enough to go all the way around your "pancake" of clay, with the coil for the first round slightly larger.

Dampen the edge of the flattened "pancake" in the bowl (which will become your base) and place your slightly larger coil around the perimeter. Support the *outside* of the coil to keep it from spreading while you smear the joint between the base and the coil with your thumb [2-3], pressing hard to make sure the seam is joined. The wooden bowl makes the base and coil easy to turn, so you can work from one spot instead of walking around and around the pot. Don't use too much water or you will soften the clay too much to support the wall. I like to work without adding any water from this point on.

Joining the coils can be done in a number of ways—but it must be done, or the dry pot will simply fall apart as the coiled layers shrink away from each other. One method is to support the coil on the inside, while pressing the outside with a fingertip, squeezing the coil onto the preceding round [2-4]. That gives you a textured outside and a smooth inside.

2-4

Another method of joining the coils is to squeeze and turn each coil slightly as it is put in place by pressing upward on the outside with your thumb and downward on the inside with your index finger [2-5]. That tends to create a smoother exterior, although it will not obliterate the coils entirely, which I find very pleasing. You don't have to disguise the fact that this piece is coil built.

As you add each coil, build a straight-sided cylinder that does not flare out over the edge of the *puki*. Then, when the bowl is as high as you want it, support the outside of the wall with one hand and begin bulging the wall outward by stroking it firmly upward and outward with the curled forefinger of your other hand against the inside of the cylinder [2-6], turning the *puki* after each couple of strokes so the wall thins evenly. You can add a little water if you need to by holding a damp sponge in the left hand on the inside of the pot. The trick is to round the pot while not destroying the pinched appearance of the outside wall.

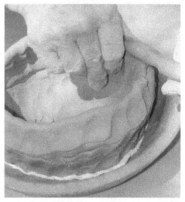

2-5

When the shape of the pot is complete, allow it to dry to leather-hardness. I sometimes cover the whole thing with plastic overnight to even out the moisture somewhat, and then take a board or the back of a wooden spoon to paddle the whole pot [2-7]. This sets the coils and gives it a finished look, although too

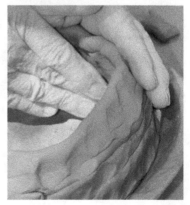

2-6

41

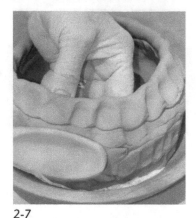

2-7

much paddling can take the character right out of a fingerprinted coiling process.

Later, if this method of coil building appeals to you, you may find that you want to knead some tempering agent (sand or grog) into the clay to stiffen it for larger shapes. *Remember:* All pots have to be fired in order to be usable for anything except holding dried weeds or the ashes of a beloved pet. Dampness will always return unfired clay to its natural state.

ASYMMETRICAL COILING

This is a variation of making a coil pot, but the point is to make an *irregular* shape. Before you begin, take a few minutes to imagine a shape that intrigues you. Seedpods may be a good place to start, or perhaps an eroded shape that caught your eye in the woods or a canyon or beside some country road. It is not necessary to have a fixed idea before you begin coiling because you will discover that the clay also has something to say about the shape that emerges.

To begin, pat out a pancake of clay about ½ inch thick. I prefer an oval or an amoeba form—anything except a perfect circle for

2-8

this shape. Put this on a board or small piece of canvas so the finished piece can be moved easily as you work.

Experiment with your coiling. Try adding a series of smaller coils that do not go all the way around the top of the shape to raise the rim or create an uneven surface [2-8]. If you have started with an irregular base, let the form emerge from there. Your design will develop as you build the shape. If a coil is placed slightly outside the preceding one, the shape will begin to flare. If it is placed slightly inside, the shape will slope inward. Pay attention to the role of moisture in what you can do with the wall of the form because too

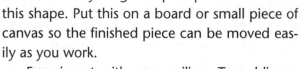

much water will cause the walls to sag, especially on these asymmetrical forms.

The shape will be stronger and have more integrity if the walls are *built* into the final shape [2-9] rather than bulging (and thinning) the form later. Inevitably, little cracks form if this is done after the wall is created, and the whole form will be weakened.

2-9

Work until the walls are *slightly* unstable, and then stop. Let the base stiffen a little if you want to continue. If you need to let your form stiffen overnight, or if you do not have time to complete it in one sitting, be sure to cover it with soft plastic. I find dry-cleaner bags work very well because they are practically weightless and will not deform the soft clay. If you are just trying to let the base stiffen and keep the working coils damp, wrap the upper third with plastic and leave the base open to dry out a bit.

Finally, the shape should be dried slowly so the coils don't shrink apart. A cool basement or some place that is protected from hot, drying wind works best. For best results, don't hurry this process.

The weight of your pot will depend on the size of the coils. Smaller pots need smaller coils. Garden containers can be built with bigger coils, but you will have to let the base dry slightly in order to hold the weight of the wet coils at the top. I have watched a Nigerian woman coil a large water jar in three hours by walking around and around the growing container as she rolled the coils between her two hands and then pinched each round in place. She was working in dry conditions, so her pot dried enough to hold the weight of the wet coils as she worked. Sometimes people use a hair dryer or small fan to stiffen the clay for a large piece. It's important not to get the base too dry, or the wet coils on top will not stick well. Your skill and sense of what the clay will allow will grow with experience.

3
Centering
A Dialogue of Discovery

I feel the whole in every part,
drawing everything in
against the wheel's disintegrating force.
My hand must be steady and true.

Centering draws the clay into a smoothly spinning mass that is evenly distributed around a central pivot point. Inside the potter's cupped hands, the clay is being mixed and remixed until all parts are smoothly joined, ready for the exuberant spread into shape that will happen next. Centering is the chamber of active nothingness, no-thingness, between the earth's long, slow work of making the clay and the human's quick work of shaping it.

To center the clay initially, the potter slams a piece of clay onto the wheel (so it will adhere firmly), and squeezes the mound of clay up and in, then down and out. It is a smooth and rhythmic motion, like slow walking or tai chi. The wheel turns every part of the clay past well-braced hands. Nothing is cut out or left protruding from the whole; all is mixed in by pressure from the potter's hands. Centering is complete when the spinning motion is not visible to the eye, and the surface feels smooth and balanced.

The technical term for the entire process between centering and finishing a piece on a potter's wheel is *throwing*, although it has nothing to do with our common image of tossing something back and forth. Throughout the entire throwing process, the potter is constantly centering, always "trueing" the pot so it does not wobble or fling an errant scrap onto the wall. From the blissful state that kneading can produce, centering moves to a focus on a particular event or form.

At the time I was learning to center a large mass of clay, M. C. Richards was writing *Centering: In Pottery, Poetry, and the Person.* Her amazing book cast the net of metaphor widely, expanding my frame of reference. Her elegant and earthy language named some of my concerns: strident individualism, restrictive public education, and narrow religious perceptions of our culture. Her work gave me language for engaging my broader concerns at the very time when I seemed to be withdrawing from the world in order to become a potter. Centering became an active way to bring it all in—my teaching in the public school, my questions about the war in Vietnam, gender questions, religious questions, my love for poetry and song, friendships, dreams, hopes. M. C. invited me to see the pottery studio as a *temenos*, a holy chamber, with centering as the primary metaphor for becoming human. She was the first to describe the soulwork of clay for me.

TOUCH

Unlike the popular image of centering as a passive meditative state, centering clay on a potter's wheel takes focus and a firm touch. Distance will not do the job. No amount of thinking will move the clay; it must be held, forced, guided, and drawn toward even distribution around the center of the spinning wheel. It takes balance and awareness, not brute strength. Centering begins with both hands placed firmly on the clay as the wheel turns. The challenge for the potter is to be able to guide the clay rather than allowing it to be bumped around if the mass is large or stiff. It is dialogue, not domination. Touch is the medium of our relationship. Inside the cocoon of clay, form is still just potential.

Physical touch brings me into the present, engages me with a sense of a living relationship between me and the clay. It is sensual and sexual, exciting and full of unknowns in a way somewhat akin to the mass of cells that will become a baby. The feel of the clay moving against my palms rescues my thoughts from diffusion and escape, calling me to confront the challenge of dealing with *this* specific piece of clay. I must be *here, now*. Difficulty demands my attention. Clay that is stiff and angular requires muscle to move it. If I try to smooth the friction by wetting my hands with water, I will soften the clay and turn it to mud—something I may regret later. So I make choices about the amount of pressure to bring, how much water to use, and the force of my being in this relationship. I must extend myself beyond comfort or passivity for the sake of something greater: the artistic impulse that is asking for form.

Centering also happens when working with clay *minus* the potter's wheel. When I am using clay in a retreat setting, I usually have people roll clay into a round ball between their hands or on a tabletop, then begin the process of shaping a pot by finding the center of the ball with one thumb while cradling the ball of clay in the other hand. Pinching proceeds from that center point by touch and feel, rather than by visual cues. It is, of course, possible to pinch a pot without centering the clay, but the most useful shapes begin with a ball shaped like the earth itself. (Directions for pinching a centered pot are included at the end of this chapter.)

On the potter's wheel, the centering process is more complex. Getting my hands dirty, moving the clay against the centrifugal force of the wheel, engages my whole self rather than just my mind. There is something so primal about the feel of wet clay and the force needed to center the clay that I am astonished by how alive I feel while centering. Nothing else that I do has this effect of engaging my whole body, breath, muscles, and mind. Putting words on a page is so clean, so abstract. Playing the piano demands dexterity, but not the kind of exertion that centering does. Even cooking rarely demands such hands-on engagement, although bread making comes closer, because it involves kneading. Gardening comes close, too, when I take off my gloves and break up the clumps of soil or mix potting soil with my hands. But when I am centering clay on the wheel, I know, deep in my bones, that we are physical creatures, fully embodied souls, meant to work and then rest.

Instead of the physical work that centering demands, our culture encourages the Greek ethos of separating body and mind—to the detriment of our souls. We become voyeurs. We treat our bodies mechanically, exercising and eating to an external standard. Our bodies then remain unconscious flesh, while our spirits become more and more detached from the consequences of our actions.

What happens to us when we do that? When we save exertion for the gym? When we trivialize handwork and say it's menial, or call it "just a hobby," instead of recognizing handwork as a sacred path to wholeness and healing? When we substitute economic gain for the soulwork of direct experience? When we accept a passive, receptive spirituality for a hands-on spirituality?

Perhaps one of the most common casualties of this mind/body separation is the way we perceive touch. We know the importance of loving touch for babies, but we seem to have forgotten that we need to give and receive touch throughout our lives. Or we've relegated touch to its sexual aspects, discounting the fact that simple caring touch keeps us healthy, alive, creative, and engaged with one another.

For the past several years, my husband, Peter, and I have led a Faith at Work summer work-pilgrimage to the highlands of Guatemala. We go to help with manual labor on a school or water project that the villagers have already chosen. And we come home with rich images of life lived in a physical, hands-on way, radically different from our technologically driven way of life. The Mayan women there wrap their babies close with a sling of brightly woven fabric that joins mother and child. Young fathers often hold the toddlers. They live close together in cornstalk huts, and touch is natural. The older children are curious, trusting, and eager to help. Even though their lives are hard, there is a sweetness and comfort of touch that comes with their way of life.

Touch reminds me that we are creatures of the earth, meant to feel deeply with our whole selves rather than just observing with eye and mind. I come back from those trips renewed and hopeful again. And clay gives me a way to extend this experience of loving touch in my daily life. When I put my hands on the wet clay and begin the centering process, I am in touch once again with the joy of knowing myself as part of all creation.

Getting in Touch

- Because we live with so much visual stimulation, it is easy to forget the power of touch. Even the simple act of consciously touching something can be a powerful way of experiencing the world, particularly for kinesthetic learners. Choose a small object that you feel attracted to and spend a few minutes with your eyes closed, touching the surface, drawing it fully into your mind and heart.

- Then put the object down and close your eyes again, keeping the object in focus. Reexperience the reality of the object as fully as you can. This is the process of conscious touch, bringing mind and hand together.

- Now, try the same thing with a piece of clay. Close your eyes so you can feel how soft or hard it is, how wet or dry it is, how warm or cold it is. Then put it down and see whether you can reexperience the same sensations simply by thinking about them.

FOCUS

During the process of centering on a potter's wheel, the clay has no particular shape, but it has mass and bulk. It has size and potential. Unlike the many possibilities of the kneading process, centering requires focus on just one. Centering invites all diversions to coalesce into a single possibility—this one piece of clay, spinning in readiness.

Centering allows us to stand in a complex field of options without being overwhelmed, staying tuned to the universe even as we go about our daily lives. It creates a kind of *kairos* moment, when the past and future join in the present moment, grounded in time and space. Centering is a dance of masculine and feminine, of *logos* and *eros*, of logic and love. It is not a balance that we come to through thought and problem solving. We find this point intuitively, beyond reason and will. We can use the focus and attentiveness of centering to act from our physical and spiritual core instead of jerking this way and that.

How easy it is to let the demands of e-mail and text messages determine who I am and what I do with my time, rather than being centered by an inner sense of my call. A daily centering practice that works for me is walking early in the morning, breathing deeply and feeling the weather changes with my whole body. The music that feeds my soul comes from birds as they begin to stir with the light. There is time to notice what's beginning to bloom or die, time to see and hear the longer swing of seasons through my neighborhood. I come back refreshed and ready for conversation at the breakfast table, plans for the day, e-mail and phone calls. My daily walk gets my whole body engaged and ready for the work ahead. Other people practice sitting or walking meditation, yoga, or other forms of body-prayer.

Finding a practice that will nurture our body-soul rhythms, as centering does, is critical for releasing creative imagination. Finding a regular time for focused centering has become more and more difficult as technology makes privacy passé. Quiet times are becoming rare. Attention to the borderland between conscious and unconscious awareness seems to be slipping away as we lose the sense of sacred wonder beneath a tide of eager acquisition. Making conscious choices to spend time in silence—taking a wellness day with the phone turned off, turning off the television an hour before bedtime, or keeping the car radio off—are simple ways to recover focus. Making choices about leisure time can also be effective: a walk in nature or a silent retreat can refresh your soul immensely.

For me, time in the pottery studio is centering time for my soul. I catch myself humming some tuneless tune of happiness and know that my soul is being fed by whatever is streaming through me. Although centering requires focus, it is an experience that extends beyond time and space. I move beyond orderly and predictable *chronos* time measured by the clock into *kairos* space, where all parts of my life are present. This isn't about "my creativity" so much as it is about entering into the long line of potters who have gone before me and will continue long after me. Time and space expand as I concentrate on the pivot point at the center. As T. S. Eliot said in his poem *Burnt Norton,* "Except for the point, the still point, there would be no dance."

We live in a culture with many options, many choices, and many activities. Distractions abound. Busyness has become a sign of success, and multitasking is a myth of increased productivity. But soul-work requires focus and wholeheartedness. To stay centered, what our minds would rather ignore must be considered, softened, and integrated. What the wheel of life would fling away needs to be contained and drawn back until the whole mass is thoroughly mixed and stabilized. Centering moves us to focused consciousness as opposing forces find their place in relation to the still point at the center.

A Clear Focus

- As a simple exercise in focusing, spend a few minutes
  exploring something familiar with your hands. You may

use your eyes for part of the exploration time, but see if you can trust your other senses to learn more about this object.

- With your eyes closed, draw the object with one continuous line, without lifting your pencil from the paper. Let the line be as long and complicated as it needs to be. Practice will improve the results and may lead to some delightful creativity as well.

DIALOGUE

Clay on the potter's wheel is not simply inert mud, waiting to be shaped by the potter's hand. The physical energy that it takes to move the clay alerts me to its nature and character, its will and wont, its glistening soul. Centering calls me to what the clay and I can do together. There are some things *this* particular piece of clay can do very well, and others that will be harder for us to accomplish together. Moving the clay up and down in the centering process lets me know how to respect the spirit of the clay and how to engage with it fully.

Centering as dialogue.

Rather than treating the clay as an "it," as just a piece of dirt, I regard the clay as the other party in a dialogue, and we begin a conversation that will bear fruit in the creative act of throwing a pot. The clay is not an extension of myself, and yet we are connected—involved in a conversation that I am just becoming conscious of.

To treat the clay as inert material, to be manipulated into a usable mass as quickly as possible, would be to miss this dance of becoming. So, too, to view other people as "objects," as predictable and static, would be to miss what Martin Buber called an "I-Thou relationship." When we

52

realize that we live in a world full of potential vibrant relationships with people and things around us, we can find that sacred spark in everything we do. This is an essential part of soulwork.

Our culture encourages us to regard people as cogs in a machine or numbers to be grouped as "target populations." So it is not surprising that we view people in front of us in line as something that slows us down. Or when we deal with customer service people over the phone, we think of them as only a means to an end.

I confess how often I live as though my life belonged to me and not some larger story, how quickly I move to what is convenient for me, forgetting that real pleasure comes from the sense of connection—on my morning walks, during a shared experience, even during a chat with the person standing in line with me. When I am too focused on myself, I quickly lose touch with delight, surprise, and celebration, forgetting that they are the fruits of dialogue.

A Centering Conversation

- Go back to the continuous line drawing that you created for the "A Clear Focus" exercise. Look at your drawing with soft eyes and an open heart, letting yourself take in the spirit of the drawing as a "holy other." Notice whether you are able to extend yourself in love toward this piece of your own creativity, to feel an I-Thou relationship with it.

- From that place of acceptance, imagine a dialogue of discovery between you and your drawing. Write about it in the privacy of a journal, if you can.

- Now take a piece of clay in your hand, and, with your eyes closed, let the clay speak to you. Does it seem to be asking for pinching or rolling or smoothing? Or might it just want to be held in stillness? If you and the clay were to have a dialogue, what might you say to each other?

Dialogue can emerge from an activity that we begin without consciousness of soulwork. Recently, I have been helping a friend clear out her mother's home in preparation for selling it. After living there for nearly fifty years, and without a mate for the last fifteen years, her mother had to move suddenly, after several small strokes. Now she is living comfortably in a single, assisted-living room, glad that we are sorting and moving her things, and yet anxious about it as well. As we began to work, it looked as though she never threw anything away. Our task became one of centering: trying to hold the threads of a family story as we made our way through pictures and records and books and utensils and all the accoutrements of success in these times. What to keep? Who might want these some day? And who might need them now? We felt the press of time, the need to get through this chaotic clutter, and yet we wanted to let this centering stage do its inner work. During this formless, in-between time, the dialogue proceeds by touch and intuition, by letting love take the lead and yet not getting lost in a morass of things.

STAYING CENTERED

Centering refers not only to the initial preparation stage of throwing a pot but also to the ongoing effort to keep the whirling mass "true" (equidistant from the still point at the center). The dance between the potter's hands and the still point must continue throughout the throwing process, making corrections as the wall thins and wobbles. The inner hand begins to define the shape of the pot, exerting more pressure to create a dynamic imbalance, while the outer hand moves in tandem, holding the circle true. It is the supportive work of one hand or the other to keep the pot anchored and true, because the very act of throwing—by putting pressure on one spot only—creates imbalance. As M. C. Richards wrote, "When we are working on the potter's wheel, we're touching the clay at only one point; and yet as the pot turns through our fingers, the whole is being affected, and we have an experience of this wholeness. 'The still point of the turning world.'"

Pressure that creates imbalance is something we are all too familiar with. On a day-to-day level, we face the pressures of schedules and bills, commitments and available energy, wishes and needs. Our "job" and our "work" (which is not always what we are paid for but may be the real reason for our job) may be opposing forces that we need to keep in balance, or they may well be like an outside hand holding and supporting the impulse of love of the inside hand. We need to center and recenter as we live with the imbalance and stimulation of dealing with a constant stream of unknowns.

As part of our mammalian heritage, we are born wanting more than food and water. A deep hunger for love runs beneath our attempts to satisfy our longings with things, accomplishments, titles, or accolades. But our culture offers plenty of substitutes, interim objects that barely hold our interest long enough to get the wrapping off. Sometimes we have become enchanted with those substitutes, mistaking goals and gimmicks for the deeper heartbeat of connection. We run and push and grab because we have lost touch with the countervailing force of centering. As social writer Eric Hoffer reminds us, *"We can never get enough of what we do not want."* Although that imbalance may result in a spectacular burst of energy or novelty, it will not last. There is not enough of the soul's DNA there to sustain it over time.

Not only does our striving for more and better throw us off balance, but also the adversities of life press in whether we are prepared or not. Illness and death come to all of us, reminding us that we live in time and that our bodies are the one mortal vessel that we have to carry through this life. Failure, whether the result of calculated risk or stubborn stupidity, can leave us quivering with fear unless we can find a countervailing source of hope. Loss happens—both in major life shifts and in the ordinary progression of change and aging. Yet even in the shambles of what was, we can find seeds of new life, if we dare to look. In the tension between what was and what is, we can recenter. If we can release the past, centering will prepare us for a future form. But if we hold on to the dried bits of earlier experience, the flow of a new form will be impeded. Leftover lumps and bubbles will destroy the possibility of a new shape, even when the foot of a new form is centered and ready on the wheel.

Although centering is a solitary discipline, a supportive community can help us keep our balance within opposing tensions. Shared values can help us stay focused, as the 12-step movement makes clear. A spiritual community can reinforce our quest for consciousness and be the place where our passions take form and help us live with the tensions that imbalance produces. Periodically, I spend a weekend with others in my church community on a silent retreat. It gives me time to rest and listen for the deeper strands of daydreams and night dreams. I usually take my journal along and sometimes read it with colored pencils or pastels in hand, letting color add a breath of life to words gone dormant with description. Going on retreat with others who are wanting to be more centered in their lives creates a kind of spiritual container for all of us. My whole being is refreshed, rested, and recentered by the experience.

For me, silent retreat is a time for poetry strung between the images of nature, for listening to the still small voice of God when storms have passed. What I *don't* need for centering is more talking, more input. To recover my relationship with the sacred still point, I need a place where my body can stretch, or sit watching a warbler sing or baby foxes playing in the sun. Observing nature without hurry gets me out of my private sphere and loosens the hold of many tasks, so I am open to the miracle of life itself. It shifts the point of my focus from "me" to the world of which I am a part. This practice of centering is a way of staying in contact with the guiding, steadying force that keeps me from flying apart on the wheel of life.

Supporting Forces

- With more and faster technologies, demands on our time can feel like the centrifugal force of the potter's wheel, flinging everything outward toward disintegration. Take a few minutes to list the inner and outer forces of your life in your journal, without judgment. Remind yourself, "These are simply the materials I have to work with."

- Centering is an integrating force, a countervailing pressure. Is there a person, a place, or an activity, such as the silent retreats I described above, that would help you stay centered? If nothing comes to mind, can you imagine what you would want or need for recentering?

- If you were to describe the shape of your life right now as a piece of clay, what would it look like?

There is another kind of centering tension that we may not recognize fully, and that is joy. It rises spontaneously when we are fully engaged, challenged to use our gifts, and supported by the right structures to put those gifts into practice. The very process of creation lifts our spirits and opens our hearts, and yet we may interpret that feeling as accomplishment, skill, or product rather than the process of centering as it unfolds. That kind of attachment to a *result* can actually drain away the joy of creativity. Our culture puts so much emphasis on productivity and problem solving that we frequently miss out on the wonder and joy that could be ours if we cultivated creativity as a spiritual practice. Henry Ward Beecher once wrote, "There are joys which long to be ours. God sends ten thousand truths, which come about us like birds seeking inlet; but we are shut up to them, and so they bring us nothing, but sit and sing awhile upon the roof, and then fly away."

Is it possible that joy and gladness could be ours from something as simple as working with clay?

Try It with Clay!

PINCHING A SMALL BOWL

Pinching a small bowl from a single piece of clay can be a centering experience, not only for the clay but for us as well. There is something powerful about the direct touch of hand on clay that evokes our deepest human longings. Pressing and stroking the clay into a thin, symmetrical bowl in time with our breathing can be a portal to peacefulness, in which we feel at one with the slower rhythms of nature.

Any clay that can be thrown on a wheel can be used for pinching a bowl. If you are purchasing clay, just ask for a body that is plastic or pliable. Because these do not have to be fired, the firing range is not important. Most people find a light-colored clay easier to use because it will not stain clothing or hands, although red clays may be more pliable and available.

Start with about ½ pound of clay, about the size of a small orange. Simply hold the ball of clay in your left hand (if you are right-handed; you will need to reverse the directions for this bowl if you are left-handed).

At workshops and on retreats, I encourage people to close their eyes as a way to trust their hands and turn off the internal critic that seems to operate so automatically in our culture. I remind them that this exercise is not about perfection—it's about experience and awareness.

We begin with breathing, relaxing, and readiness. When the room is quiet and everyone is settled comfortably in a chair, I say something like this:

> *Breathe in the sounds and smells of this room, this time,*
> *   this place ...*
> *Breathe out what you do not need to be here now.*

Breathe in the feel of your body, balanced and steady ...
Breathe out your thoughts, so you can be here now.
As you breathe in, let your breath go to your belly ...
As you breathe out, release any tensions you feel.
Now continue to breathe easily, naturally,
> *with your hands cupped open to receive your piece of*
> *clay.*

Then, as I move from person to person, I put a piece of clay about the size of an orange in their cupped hands and remind them softly, "This is our body. Let your hands explore the clay tenderly, as you would the face of a friend."

As you hold your ball of clay, you might want to use some of these suggestions to help you breathe and relax as you explore the clay.

When you are ready to begin, press down in the center of your ball of clay with your right thumb and squeeze the clay gently between your thumb and the curled knuckle of that same hand resting on the outside of the clay [3-1]. Rotate the ball slowly after each press, squeezing the clay lightly as you rotate the ball. Continue this motion until you have created an opening the size of your thumb that goes down to about ¼ inch from the bottom of the ball. The goal is to have clay evenly distributed around the pivot point under your thumb.

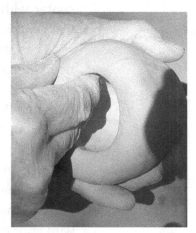

3-1

Then begin to spread the bottom of the bowl with your thumb without widening the top opening, rotating the ball after each stroking motion. From the widening base, begin to pinch the clay wall, and then turn the bowl slightly with your other hand as you work your way up the wall in a slow spiral. As you approach the top rim, lessen the pressure from your thumb and increase the pressure from your knuckle on the outside in order thicken the rim, which will help hold the overall shape. Try to keep the top rim from spreading or cracking. If it does, you may be working with too much pressure. Try making more, smaller pinches as you get the feel of the clay.

I like to remind people to keep their eyes closed while they breathe and pinch, breathe and pinch, slowing down the process.

Then it's time to work on the rim. You can thicken the rim by supporting it on both sides with the thumb and forefinger of your left hand, and pressing down with the pad of your right index finger. Do not add water because that tends to thin out the rim and will increase shrinkage later. A slightly thicker rim will help hold the bowl round and give it a sense of definition.

Variation: Pinching a Larger Bowl

For this project, you will need 1 pound of clay. Begin as you would with a smaller amount of clay, by rolling it into a ball, finding its center with your thumb, opening the bottom, and pinching the walls without spreading the top rim too much.

Then shift your attention to working on just the top half of the bowl. Keep the bottom of the bowl damp with a piece of plastic wrap inside and out so you will be able to thin and reshape it later to match the contour of the top half. Even though the bottom may tend to flatten and thicken if you are working on a table, you can correct that later.

Experiment with using your thumb on the outside and your fingers on the inside as you lengthen and spread the top half of the pot into the shape you want. If you support the shoulder of the pot with your fingers inside, your thumb will naturally flatten the shoulder, and it will be easier to control the thickness and size of the rim. With your thumb on the inside of the pot, the rim will tend to flare outward. Remember to breathe, keeping your eyes closed.

When the top half feels uniformly pinched, it is time to open your eyes and behold your creation with an open heart. You may need to consciously resist critiquing your work. Instead, take a few minutes just to hold it in your hands and feel its wholeness.

When you are satisfied with the upper half of the bowl and the rim, let it stiffen until it is leather-hard. When the rim is stiff enough to hold the bowl in shape, remove the plastic wrap from the bottom half. Cup the bowl in one hand and use the fingers of the other hand inside to stretch the clay and lengthen the form without distorting the rim. As you come to the end of making this bowl, take a minute to sit with it in both hands, breathing and knowing it by touch, and letting yourself feel whatever feelings your creation evokes.

Finally, invert the bowl so it is resting on its rim to let the bottom half of the bowl stiffen. When the base is leather-hard, tap the bottom of the bowl gently on a table to create a simple flat foot.

If you are interested in a more detailed description of pinching a small begging bowl, along with many variations on that basic shape, I recommend Paulus Berensohn's fine book *Finding One's Way with Clay: Pinched Pottery and the Color of Clay*.

PINCHING A LONG VASE

Once you have mastered the technique of pinching a small bowl, you might try a larger piece of clay. Instead of holding and rotating the clay in one hand and pinching with the other, you can turn the clay on its side so it is resting on one hand in your lap while you draw it out toward the rim with the fingers of your other hand, taking care not to let the opening get too large. As the pot lengthens, you may find yourself supporting the clay with your hand and forearm while the fingers of your other hand reach in and draw the clay outward, toward the rim, stroking the clay rather than pinching it, as you were able to do on the smaller bowl.

When you have finished the rim and upper portion of the pot, you can "hang" the pot on your fist, continuing to stroke it downward toward the rim from the outside. You might put a paper towel around your fist and arm to help you slide the elongated form off easily.

3-2

3-3

3-4

To make the pot rounder, you can hold it in your lap and stroke the clay outward from the inside, taking care to support and compress it from the outside with your other hand. If you do not support it from the outside, the pot will tend to develop cracks on the outer surface. If the inner surface is smooth (because you are stroking the clay there), exterior cracks will not hurt the pot and can be a decorative surface.

MAKING A CLAY BALLOON

Trapping air inside of a closed clay "balloon" is another way to create an interesting and stable form that will withstand a fair amount of pressure from the outside.

Begin by pinching two small bowls of roughly equal size and diameter [3-2].

It is important that the rims be even, so you may need to trim off slight variations with a pair of scissors. To do that, place the bowl on a small piece of paper towel so it can be turned easily. Then brace your arm so the scissors will remain level, and turn the bowl as you trim it evenly all around. Then roughen the edges of each bowl with a fork and press them together, taking care not to indent the seam or deform the bowls [3-3]. Adding water will weaken the wall, so avoid that if possible. A small coil of clay can be pressed over the seam to make sure the form is airtight.

If, in handling the two halves, an indentation has occurred [3-4], you can make a small hole and blow into the clay balloon until it swells outward again, then close the hole by pinching it with your lips or inserting a small plug of clay.

Once the seam is tight, you can play with texturing the outside. Don't worry about your "balloon" popping, because the air trapped inside will support the whole piece. You can roll your balloon on rocks or moss, wrap it with string or grass, paddle the outside with a wooden spoon, texture it with your fingers, or experiment with pressing different objects into the surface.

Finally, after the clay balloon has stiffened a little, you will need to finish it by pricking the surface with a pin to let the air escape, or it will crack open as the clay shrinks. You can also add a neck by shaping one with your fingers and attaching it as you did the coil around the middle. You can then open a larger hole through the neck into the air-locked cavity with a pencil.

A "Clay Balloon" Story

When a friend of ours died recently, her husband wanted to take a portion of her ashes with us on a pilgrimage to Guatemala, where they had shared a deeply satisfying work experience. We talked about how to transport her ashes through customs, and I thought of using this technique of "clay balloons" to make closed clay forms, because they are so stable. I invited him and his two daughters to join me on the back deck to make four small containers out of clay for her ashes. There was something simple and satisfying about sitting together, talking quietly as each of us pinched both halves of a balloon, then joined them with a coil.

When they were dry, the four small containers resembled eggs. We sanded the surface of each "egg," and then decorated them with water-based paints, adding words and designs to the smooth, rounded surface. When we were done, I drilled a small hole in one end of each egg with a sharp knife, and we poured my friend's ashes into each one, using a funnel through the small opening. I then plugged each one with a clay patch secured with vinegar (which doesn't shrink as much as water).

For the trip to Guatemala, my friend's husband simply wrapped one of the eggs in a plastic bag and packed it in his suitcase, surrounded by his clothes. It survived the trip with no damage, but when we got to Lake Atitlán, a severe thunderstorm interrupted our planned service. We huddled under a tin roof as lightning flashed and the rain pounded overhead, until, as we were ready to leave, the sun broke through the rain clouds just at the horizon and a stillness beckoned us to continue. We sang and prayed at the water's edge with flowers and candles, held our simple service as the waves continued to pitch and toss, and finally deposited my friend's "egg" in the water—where it would dissolve with her ashes. Although I thought the flowers would be tossed back to the shore by the waves, they floated away into the dying sunlight as lightning jerked along the skyline and darkness descended.

The next morning dawned bright and clear. When we checked the shoreline, only a few puddles of wax remained in the sand where our candles had burned down. The water was calm and clear. There was no sign of the egg or my friend's ashes. Her body had returned to the earth, and a new day began for her and for all of us.

3-5

PINCHING SHAPES

Another way of pinching clay is NOT to start with a round ball, but to let your pinching follow the shape of the clay as it comes to you. Practice breathing and working with your eyes closed without centering the clay, and notice how much you can know about the clay just by feel [3-5].

Sometimes our hands have something in mind that emerges only when we stop giving directions, telling them what to do. Try sitting with a small piece of clay, and distract your mind by counting your breaths as you let your hands play with the clay.

Or you could begin to pinch a piece of clay with a specific image in mind:

- A letter to a friend
- A gift for someone who has died
- A longing of your heart
- A song or a poem
- A family outing
- A secret treasure

As the shape emerges, ask yourself whether there is anything that the clay has told you about the image you have been holding. You may want to write down your conversation with the clay, or create a poem from your dialogue.

PINCHING SCULPTURES

The exercise of making a figure from a single piece of clay can lead to whimsical sculptures as well as powerful iconic images. For some reason, people tend to build a sculptural piece by adding pieces of clay, which inevitably dry apart and drop off. It's much better to start with a modest ball about the size of an orange, and pinch it into a shape without adding anything more.

You might observe a household pet, such as a dog or cat, and try to catch the sense of its whole body curled in sleep in your clay. Try pinching five quick studies of this resting animal. (You may want to use one for your "soul space," if you created one in the first chapter.)

You can expand your range of observation with photographs. Sometimes I look through a copy of *National Geographic* to find an animal that intrigues me and try this pinching exercise to see whether I can turn a flat image into a three-dimensional figure with clay. The sculpture pictured in figure 3-6 was made by Jean Mideke,

3-6

3-7

my teacher Louie's wife. Quite often, my efforts to pinch an animal turn into mythical beasts, as I see how limited my powers of observation and memory really are!

Another source for studies in pinching might be your vegetable bin. Try using a tomato as a model. Or a green pepper. An apple or a pear. Or several chile peppers in a pile.

On the windowsill above my kitchen sink, there is a small black angel that I pinched absent-mindedly one time while I was meditating with a small piece of clay in my hands. I had not intended to make anything, but she arrived anyway, with a lap that has held many small things—a shell, a bead, a tiny charm. That day, I had begun my meditation in a very agitated state, unable to find a centered place in breath or body. I was sitting cross-legged, with the weight of a ball of clay cupped in my hands like a sinker—hoping it would anchor me somehow. As I focused on my breathing, my fingers began to move on the clay, unbidden. My hands must have shaped this small figure [3-7], because she was there when I opened my eyes to see what my hands had made while my mind was counting my breaths. When she had dried, I tucked her into a bowl for protection, and nestled her into a sawdust firing.

Variation: Larger Figures

At this point, we are working with raw clay that will simply dry and hold its shape. This means it is possible to pinch larger sculptural figures from a single piece of clay for firing (which we will get to in chapter 7). If you want to try this, you may need to add sand or another tempering agent to help your figure survive the firing process. Too much sand will reduce its plasticity and make it harder to shape, but too little may result in it sagging under the weight of wet clay. If the piece is to be fired, you must hollow out thick, solid parts of your sculpture to keep it from cracking as the surface clay shrinks in drying.

Although Jean Mideke used photos to create her sculpture of a polar bear pictured at right [3-8], her firsthand experience of living along the Kobuk River in Alaska, during the years when Louie was a gold miner, clearly helped bring this image to life. This 12-inch-high sculpture was bisque fired and not glazed (I'll discuss bisque firing in chapter 7).

3-8

4
Shaping
Inner and Outer Pressures Dance Together

Opening the centered mound
creates space for the inner hand
to press against the outer
at a single point
on the moving wall.

Everything conspires to keep the clay of our lives closed and contained. We tell ourselves that a scheduled life and a gated community means we will be safe and secure, buffered from risk by policies and programs, even though these give no breathing room to our souls. But the truth is, new life demands space.

If I am working on a potter's wheel, as the closed mound of clay spins, I press my thumb downward at the still point to open the way for thrust from the inside. Opening the mound of centered clay allows one hand to work on the inside cavity while the other presses back through the clay, thinning and shaping the wall of each pot. Once that has happened, the inside space opens easily, surging outward with the speed of the wheel toward shape and form in the world. If I am pinching a bowl, I create that inner space by holding the ball of clay in one hand and pressing the clay between thumb and curled forefinger of the other hand. From the beginning of recorded time, that's the way simple bowls were made—form defined by its inner space.

Shaping a pot is a folk dance of opposing pressures. At first, the clay feels dense and heavy footed, centered solidly on the wheel. Then, from inside and outside, both hands work together in creating the pot, leaning and swirling around the center point until the outside shape mirrors the inner space. The amazing properties of clay—pliability and the capacity to hold its shape—come alive in this throwing process.

OPENING

Cupping my hands around the mass of spinning clay, I find the center point with my thumbs, pressing down while the wheel does the work centrifugally, flinging the clay outward. Then, filling the well I have created with water to keep the clay pliable, I pull a thick ring of clay outward, where it will be used to make the entire wall of the pot. The speed of the wheel helps with this expanding movement. What I think of as the spirit-space of the pot expands naturally with the outward thrust of the wheel, swelling like an infant taking its first full breath. The pot seems alive now.

Once opened, my inner hand works by feel, pressing outward in an upward spiral to define the inner shape of the pot. At the same time, my outer hand applies strong counterpressure, guiding the clay inward to keep the spinning mass from flinging itself off the wheel. I brace my outer hand, elbow to knee, so my whole body becomes a centering force. Sometimes, if I have put too much water on the surface in an attempt to keep the clay sliding smoothly between the friction of my opposing fingers, a fine slurry of clay sprays everything in its path. Moist and smooth and moving, the clay feels muscular. We resist each other, body to body, as I move the clay into a fat ring on the wheel head, expanding the spirit-space inside. It is full of potential.

All of us have this inner vitality, this soul-force, this energetic *eros*, pressing outward against people and structures, and it makes us who we are. James Hillman, in his book *The Soul's Code: In Search of Character and Calling,* describes how the essence of each person is there from the beginning. This soul-force is strongly visible in preschool children before they have been tamed by the systems of school and church and work demands. With luck and intention, each soul becomes conscious and grows into its unique shape or form in the world.

Opening must be encouraged and supported at each stage of life. Sometimes external forces are too strong, and they threaten to overwhelm the soul's life force. A teenage friend of ours recently emerged from a terrifying bout with anorexia, which had fixated her attention on perfection and control of her food intake to the point of starvation. Fortunately, her soul rebelled, assisted by caring parents and medical staff. The life force within her was stronger than those external messages of thinness as perfection. When she sat down with me at a church potluck, her plate piled high with salad, she announced vehemently, "When I'm fifty, I'm going to eat anything I want!" The energy behind her words let me know that she was finding a new balance, feeling her desire for food and making healthy choices—something we all need to learn in our many-options society. I suspect she was also saying that, by age fifty (which must seem like eternal old age to her), she would feel at home in her body, so her wants and desires would be congruent with her body image—something she did not feel at fifteen.

Opening up space for our souls to thrive means different things at different ages. The soulwork of young adulthood is to develop a healthy ego, strong enough to make good decisions in the midst of a culture based on external appearances and economic power. But as we approach midlife, our soulwork changes. The pulse of *eros* shifts as we begin to understand our lives in a broader, more mysterious universal context that includes death. Love broadens to include our broken and banished parts. The inner hand finds new and more subtle shapes to express, as competence gives way to compassion.

When I work with older adults who have never touched clay and do not have access to a potter's wheel, I often invite them to work with clay using a "paddling" method. Because they sometimes lack the strength or dexterity to shape the clay manually, "paddling" is a very accessible technique. It involves opening the clay by pressing your fist into a grapefruit-size ball of clay, and then propping your elbow up on the table so the clay hangs down over your fist. As you pat the clay with the back of a wooden spoon or paddle, while turning the clay, the clay stretches downward. In fact, it is quite possible to make a sizable pot this way, in one or two sittings. (Paddling is a fun technique; I've included some projects at the end of the chapter so you can try it.)

Paddling is also a great metaphor. It suggests that outer pressures sometimes come as a strike or blow against the clay of our lives, rather than intentional pressure from human expectations. There are blows that affect us, stretch and shape us from the outside simply because we are alive and can respond by holding steady, like a braced forearm. Opening needs to happen again and again throughout our lives, whenever external pressures threaten to close in around our souls.

Opening Up Soul Space

- Can you recall a time when something happened to you, or to someone close to you, that opened up a new sense of your inner life, your soul-force? Perhaps there was an illness, or a move, when the usual external supports were suddenly removed. Or a new opportunity that called for all of your resources, for everything you ever knew, and more besides.

- If you imagine your inner life as a series of containers, what would those shapes be? You might create a timeline and use line drawings to describe your inner shapes at different stages of your life.

EQUALIZING

Pulling a cylinder is the term used for the next step of formation on a wheel, although the potter is not actually pulling or tugging the clay into shape. After opening the clay and pressing a flat bottom firmly against the wheel with my thumbs, I take a deep breath, as though preparing to dive into a pool. I dampen the clay, inside and out, using a sponge so I can put the water exactly where my fingers will be touching the clay. Too much water will collect in the bottom or spin off the wheel onto everything (including my lap).

Equalizing the pressure between my hands, I start to pull the clay upward in a long, slow spiral of pressure, a single fingertip on the inside braced against my curved knuckle on the outside of the clay wall. Matching pressure inside and out is important for maximum stability as the wall begins to climb vertically between my fingers. The outer visible hand must be sensitive to the pressure of the inside hand, the speed of the wheel, and the softness of the clay. I concentrate on that single point of tension where my fingers on either side of the wall are nearly touching through the clay. That is where change happens.

With each pull—for it will take several to stretch the clay as high as I want it to go—I need to breathe and stay centered myself. As a metaphor, pulling a cylinder mirrors our need to match inner and outer life pressures. I think of the inner, less visible hand as the expression of creative energy in me, what I understand as the sexual, sensual pulse of *eros*. It is full of feeling and intuition. The outer hand is more like my rational side, the *logos* of thought and word, calculating where more water or pressure is needed to keep the clay centered and keep the pot true. It might seem that the outward hand determines the shape— just as we tend to look at outward appearances in

Pulling a cylinder.

73

our culture—but pulling a cylinder tells me that *eros* and *logos* must be balanced.

For most of us, outer pressures are fairly obvious. Work and family exert the pressures of roles and responsibilities, and the pressures of other people's demands and expectations can sometimes make us feel trapped. Inner pressures are not so obvious, particularly if we have been schooled to think of others first. If we try single-handedly to maintain inner space and time for soulwork, it may not be enough to counterbalance the external pressure.

Sometimes organizational structures can help us anchor our inner life. When Peter and I first arrived in Washington, D.C., my inner sense of call—to reclaim the unity of body, mind, and spirit—had been nurtured by clay for a decade. But at that point, I was unsure of the shape I wanted to be as I approached midlife. I found encouragement at Seekers, a small lay-led church birthed out of Church of the Saviour. The first time we attended, I wept to see a man and a woman celebrating Eucharist together at the altar. This was at a time when most churches were still caught in a patriarchal pattern of male hierarchy, and my soul was crying for attention in the sacred spaces of my life. To see that partnership of equals at the altar gave me a visible sign that Seekers could be a place where my soul's longing for expression would be welcomed. I took that sign as a nudge from my soul that this would be a safe place to learn and grow.

From the beginning, Seekers gave me a place to try out new things, to expand and grow as an artist, an author, a teacher, and a preacher. There was plenty of room to experiment with creative liturgy, chant and drama, fasting and foot washing, and oddball high jinks, such as liturgical clowning. There was a marvelous spirit of inventiveness, along with a real generosity of time and money for social justice issues. The expectation at Seekers—intentional deepening of one's inner and outward spiritual journey—helped nourish my inner life. Peter and I were fed and watered and cared for like the spiritual newborns that we were when we arrived.

Meanwhile, the external pressures for "pulling the cylinder" of my life came in the vocational realm. When Peter came to the end of his first career in the Army, I began to look for work that would be a more public expression of my soulwork with clay. That took me to seminary, and then to Faith at Work, a relational ministry not associated with any religious denomination. We had been receiving the *Faith at Work* magazine for many years and had attended several of their leadership training events, and I had been volunteering as the coordinator of their Women's Ministry while attending seminary. I also knew that the ministry was in serious financial straits when the magazine ceased publication, and I began to think that I might be able to help the organization find a new form.

When I was offered the position as president of Faith at Work, the organization was like a spinning mass of clay. It seemed barely centered, and yet it was ready to be opened. Later, I learned from the board treasurer that the selection committee figured that Faith at Work had a life expectancy of about three years, more or less. I had, in some ways, been hired to close the place down—except that I didn't know it. I saw our financial challenges as an opportunity to open the organization to new ways of operating, even as we (the board, staff, and I) struggled to stay centered in what we understood of God's call or purpose. Very quickly I realized that the external pressures of work were so strong that I would have to deepen my inner life at Seekers in order to maintain any sense of balance. Equalizing those pressures felt like learning to walk before I could dance.

Opposing Forces

- Take a few minutes to make a line drawing of your body. Use color to identify the external pressures that you feel and where they might be impacting your body. Are there areas where external pressures are concentrated? Or are

75

they spread around your whole body? Be as particular as you can be about those external pressures.

• Then use another color to identify any internal pressures you feel. These are likely to be feelings of joy or sadness, anger or special aliveness. Notice whether they counteract the external pressures, or whether they are located in another part of your body entirely.

• Take some time to reflect on your drawing and ask what it reveals about the shaping pressures in your life right now.

INTENTIONAL IMBALANCE

Although equal pressure is the goal when pulling a cylinder, imbalance is essential at the end for good design. As shaping continues, there comes a time to *unbalance* my touch and let one hand or the other predominate in order to curve the form into a pleasing shape. More pressure from my inner hand will flare the pot outward with the wheel's motion. Pressure from my outer hand will turn the wall inward, thickening and constricting the shape at the belly, shoulder, or neck. At this point, the final form emerges quickly with each pull. As the wall gets thinner, my options narrow because certain moves cannot be reversed without collapsing the entire form. Each decision, each direction, makes a difference. Close attention at the point of contact through the clay creates a kind of intimacy as I explore the clay's increasing thinness and elasticity with more clarity about its final form.

Imbalance is the essence of this stage of the dance because unequal pressures determine the line and flow of the shape. Extension, suspension, and movement swirl around a still point at the center to create a unique piece. Soulwork demands this focused tension and intention in our daily lives, where everything conspires to keep these inner and outer pressures from creating a shape together. In our culture, we are frequently taught to avoid tension, if possible. We tend to work in one environment and reserve spiritual practices for home, to relieve the stress in private, rather than developing a disciplined inner life to push back against cultural forces. We are lulled into thinking that we are "living the good life" when we can sustain external signs of success. And although we may be aware of wanting to tend our spirits, we often don't know how. Soulwork may seem like a good thing, but we just don't seem to have the time. Or we shy away from too much introspection, too much attention to spiritual matters. But conscious soulwork requires that we bring these countervailing pressures together, holding the tension with precision and clarity.

When I am throwing a pot, I am frequently surprised to find that I am holding my breath a little, as though waiting to see what possibilities the clay has hidden from my earlier touch. At the same time, I have learned to trust the clay's capacity for expansion and change. With intimacy and trust comes love for this clay vessel as it takes shape in my hands.

And so it was with my work. When, after three years, we had not only made Faith at Work survive but had also gotten the magazine back into print, I let love and a certain amount of foolishness be my guide. In the beginning, I was so embarrassed by the look and feel of the little magazine we were able to produce that I couldn't imagine charging anything for it. So the board decided to offer it for free and ask people to make a contribution to cover costs, if they could. Surprisingly, that worked!

Every issue felt like another pot, shaped inside and out by trembling hands. I had no training as a journalist or publisher, and our volunteer editorial board was dedicated but inexperienced. We were hanging on by a thread, and yet people kept sending articles. Enough money came in to keep publishing, and gradually the financial picture stabilized enough to expand the magazine and make it a quarterly. In my role as editor and publisher, I was like a potter, exploring each issue to feel where the thin spots were, letting one hand or the other adjust the pressure to create something with a sense of movement and surprise. Working with intentional imbalance began to feel like dancing, which is about movement rather than lasting perfection. Regular deadlines shifted our focus toward doing the best we could with each issue and moving on, because there would always be another chance. That felt like pushing back against the *logos* demand for perfection as an ideal.

Tensions

- Where do you feel extended or stretched to the breaking point? Is it because of your own desires or ambitions, or a sense of inner push? Or does it come from outside demands, roles, or institutions?

- Where is the tension point or points between your inner life and your outer pressures?

- Is there a central reference point for you? Something that helps you "make sense" of the pressures inside and out? Often we need a community to help us hold the inner space in our lives. Where do you get that support?

CONGRUENCE

Good design calls for integrity and congruence between the inside space and the outer form. When I make pots, I want the "look" and the "feel" to match. While I work, I like to watch the outline of my clay take shape in a mirror that sits directly in front of my wheel. I also "watch" with my fingers deep inside the cavity that grows as the clay is stretched and shaped. I feel for integrity between external appearance and the pot's soul-shape. If a pot is thick in some places and thin in others, uneven shrinkage during drying or firing may cause cracks to develop. Then the pot's potential is quite different from what it would have been as an evenly thin pot. When I am throwing well, congruence is not a question I have to struggle with.

It simply happens. The clay seems to sing and settle into its own shape, reflecting the inside shape of my imagination in the visible outer skin.

As I come to the end of the shaping process, specific details become more important: Should the neck be more defined? The shoulder lifted? The belly rounded? These details give each pot character and identity. I have to trust my sense of the whole piece to tell me when the shaping is done, when a pot is congruent inside and out. That doesn't necessarily mean it will be "pretty" in a conventional sense, but I believe that good design is functional and satisfying. My pottery mentor, Louie Mideke, used to say, "Take care of the foot and the lip, and the middle will take care of itself." That applies not only to pottery but also to any creative endeavor with inner and outer pressures. If we pay attention to centering and opening well, and plan for good closure at the end, the middle will have its own shape and integrity.

Why do some pots seem lifeless and others full of soul? It is surely not symmetry. I've seen Korean tea bowls, deceptively simple in shape and size, that seem redolent with soul, and others that seem mechanical in their perfection. This is the same mystery we see in human beings: some people fully inhabit their lives, and others seem like living shells, almost robotic. Congruence is a matter of integrity where the outside matches the inside.

When I was a teenager, I used to practice the pipe organ at a mortuary, where I shared the space with many different people who had died. None looked alive, no matter how carefully they had been "prepared" for viewing. The mysterious life force that we associate with breath or spirit was missing. That experience left me with a dualistic sense of body as being separate from spirit. But clay brought me to a more complex understanding of soulfulness as a *quality of the body itself*. Perhaps it is the divine dimension of matter waiting for consciousness. Perhaps what we recognize as soulfulness in music or art, pottery or person, is the sacred spark of our common Source. Creativity is born of congruence and a willingness to live with imbalance, with uneven forces inside and out.

Congruence is part of staying centered throughout the process, of feeling the whole in every part. As thin spots emerge, we must use a lighter touch and not panic, but stay engaged and alert to the central purpose. To me, that is an essential part of soulwork.

When I started my position with Faith at Work, a potential "thin spot" was the fear some people had that I would turn the organization into a women's ministry. As more women were stepping into places of public leadership, those fears were surfacing in many institutions. Although I had been part of the push by women for more leadership roles in Faith at Work, I promised myself that I would work for equity and balance for men and women. I made sure that male authors were featured in every issue of the magazine, that events included men at least half the time, and that the board included able, dedicated men as well as women. It was a tension that brought more creativity, not less. In the magazine, we selected a wide variety of authors—some experienced writers and some not. In an effort to invite a broad participation, the regular columnists acted as scouts, encouraging new people to write. Although we didn't pay for articles, we could promise them an interested audience of some twenty thousand readers. Because we had no advertisers and were not associated with any particular religious denomination, we found our way through doctrinal disputes with a minimum of fuss.

Congruence came from my attention to sharing the "soft clay" of my vulnerability with a few others, so that the inner pressures of my soul and my soul-community at Seekers could be brought to bear on the outer pressures of my work. There were a few particular people who noticed my struggles to be faithful at work, who asked and cared. Sonya Dyer, one of the founders of Seekers Church, came to my office periodically just to learn about the concerns I was carrying there. My weekly mission group gave me a place to share my inner life, struggles, and questions, and to offer something back to our community through teaching and preaching. More important, our weekly worship reminded me of the larger stories that gave meaning to my particular questions—the biblical story and the longer story of creation. Both were celebrated and named in music, art, and words each week. That was the bigger context I needed to gain a wider perspective on in my personal concerns.

The Whole Picture

- Do you feel satisfied with the match between your inner capacities and your outer activities?

- Are there things you need or want to adjust to bring more congruence between your inner life and its outer form?

- What are some steps you might take in that direction?

At the beginning of shaping, opening the clay means that there is more *clay* than *form*—the pot is mostly potential. Pulling a cylinder, with even pressures inside and out, begins to spread the clay, thinning and stretching it as the wall climbs and the inner space grows. Then, when it is time for the final shape, imbalance must be sustained in relationship to the still point at the center of the spinning mass. If the inner pressure is stronger, the pot balloons out. If the outer pressure is stronger, the form will constrict and thicken. Both hands must feel the whole at the point of tension, sustaining the pull rather than leaving it to wobble off the axis. Finally, congruence is a mark of the potter's skill—when the outer shape accurately reflects the inner space. That is a sign of integrity.

Try It with Clay!

A PADDLED POT

For this exercise, you will need a paddle of some sort. A heavy wooden spoon works just fine for this, or you can purchase or make a small wooden paddle. Even a bottle with a long neck to hold on to will work. You will also need some smooth, rounded stones.

Begin with a round ball of clay about the size of a grapefruit. Put the ball on a paper towel or a small cloth—something to keep it from sticking to the table surface—and place your curled fist firmly in the center of the ball, pressing it down into the clay. With each press, turn the clay so you keep a relatively even ring of clay around your fist as the hole deepens. Leave about a ½ inch of thickness for the bottom, because it will tend to thin out during your paddling.

Once the initial hole is made, I like to cover my fist with a paper towel to keep it from sticking to the inside of the pot as I paddle. Then I prop my elbow on the table and "hang" the clay on my left fist while I paddle it on the outside with a small board, wooden spoon, or other smooth surface [4-1].

Paddling is another way of moving the clay in a direction, so I usually start by thinning out the middle of the ring of clay. I tap the clay smartly in a downward direction (toward my elbow) and then turn it so I am thinning the entire midsection of the pot all the way around. As with pinching, it is important to paddle and turn, paddle and turn, so the wall of the clay is being thinned evenly.

You may be surprised by how much your hand inside the clay can tell about the clay cylinder as it grows downward over your wrist and forearm. You can feel the thickness of the wall and detect any thin spots that may develop around your fist by the weight of the wall. If you do feel a thin spot developing, you can concentrate your paddling on thicker spots, or you can remove the clay from your hand and let it stiffen a bit. Sometimes soft clay moves too easily and the unevenness of your knuckles creates a thin spot if you do not keep rotating the clay often enough.

Once the clay has been lengthened to the height you want, you can remove it from your fist and tap the rim on the table to even the rim and thicken it slightly. Do not worry if the walls and base of the pot are thicker and straighter than you want, or if the inside is uneven. This can be corrected later when some of the water has evaporated and the clay is stiffer.

When the rim has hardened enough to hold its shape, hold the pot in your lap. I find that a simple apron helps give the pot a resting place while I use both hands for shaping. Then hold a smooth stone on the inside of the pot and paddle on the outside with your right hand (reverse, if you are left-handed). The stone will give you a firm smooth surface on the inside of the pot.

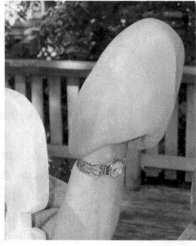

4-1

Working slowly and patiently, begin rounding the pot by paddling against the stone, turning the pot each time so you are thinning the clay evenly all the way around. Work on the top half of the pot first, from the middle and upward, toward the rim. Notice that you are actually stretching the clay out and toward the rim with your paddle strokes rather than hitting the clay squarely. The curve of the stone and the curve of your paddle will have some influence on the effectiveness of your paddle strokes. Flatter surfaces on either side increase the amount of contact area and will leave a trail of flat facets on the wall of the pot.

To finish the bottom half of the pot, you can rest the pot on your knees and work horizontally, paddling up from the base to the midsection as you move the stone on the inside of the pot to meet the paddle's impact [4-2]. Remember to

4-2

repeat your paddle strokes all the way around the pot at each section, rotating the pot frequently as though you were paddling one coil at a time.

Round pots of great beauty and delicacy can be made this way. You can complete the basic shape during the first session. Then invert the pot and loosely wrap it with plastic to allow some drying to occur before a second round of thinning (by paddling) completes the shape. This is when you can correct whatever lumps and bumps you left during the initial shaping.

Sometimes it is the imperfect roundedness of a form that makes it feel alive. Because we live in a culture where machine-made perfection is the norm, there is something very satisfying and very human about embracing the out-of-round shapes that emerge in spite of our best efforts. Japanese tea connoisseurs are said to prefer the aliveness of Korean peasant tea bowls because they are *wabi-sabi,* "not too perfect."

Variation: Asymmetrical Pot

Since using the stone inside creates a solid support for the paddle's action on the outside of the pot, you can also let the pot swell and breathe like the curve of a body. Once you have mastered the art of making a round pot with this method, experiment with asymmetrical forms.

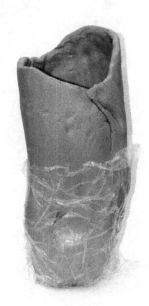

For the pot pictured [4-3], I "hung" the clay on my fist and braced my elbow on the table so I could keep turning the cylinder as it lengthened toward my elbow, paddling downward (toward the rim). Because the rim is not even, I could not rest it on the rim to let it stiffen, so I wrapped the base in plastic to keep it moist and let the top half stiffen before continuing. Later, I unwrapped the base and continued to lengthen it with more paddling.

4-3

84

You can also experiment with shaping by laying a long cylinder on a flat surface, supporting it on the inside with a board, and flattening the shape with your paddle [4-4]. Notice that the base of this next piece has been smoothed so it will stand without tipping.

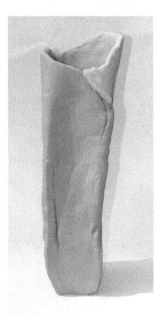

4-4

THROWING A PLATE

Making a flat plate by centering a ball of clay and then putting all the shaping pressure on the inside surface is harder than it looks. If you have access to a potter's wheel, you will need to have a plaster or Masonite bat on the wheel for this exercise because it is impossible to lift a flat plate off the wheel without deforming it.

Experiment with centering the clay, opening a hole in the center, and then putting all the pressure on the inside of the shape, drawing it out toward the rim of the wheel. Moving the clay evenly can be done with one hand braced by the other, or with both hands moving the collar of clay out toward the rim. The trick is to control the thickness of the plate. If it is too thick, the wide, flat surface will dry and curl upward from the rim, pulling a crack into the body of the plate. If it is too thin, there is the danger that your cutting wire will climb toward the center of the plate and cut a hole in it as you try to separate the clay from the throwing surface.

If you are working on a plaster bat, the bat will absorb enough moisture from the bottom of the plate to separate it when you invert the plate onto a flat surface—the way you would turn a layer cake out of its pan. You can make a plaster bat by following the directions on the box of plaster to make a thick mixture of plaster and water, then pouring it into a glass pie pan so there will be no seams or impressions. Then you can fix your plaster bat to the wheel head with some clay slurry and release it with a simple pry tool, such as a spatula.

If you are working on a Masonite bat, you will need to use a cutting wire to remove the plate. Make a deep groove around the base of the plate with a wooden tool to keep the cutting wire close to the bat. Place your cutting wire in the groove, hold it with one hand firmly against the wheel and turn the wheel slowly as you draw the other end of the cutting wire toward you. Anchoring one end will help keep the cutting wire from climbing up in the middle and cutting the center out of your plate.

In his later years, Pablo Picasso used greenware (unfired clay) plates to create fabulous paintings on clay. You, too, can experiment with design and texture on a flat clay surface by using watercolors on greenware, whether you fire your plates or not.

THROWING A CLOSED FORM

If making a plate requires pressure on the *inside* of a centered mound of clay, throwing a closed form requires more pressure on the *outside*. A closed form, such as the pinched "clay balloon" described in chapter 3, is useful because the trapped air will act as an internal support so you can deform or texture the outer surface without collapsing the walls.

4-5

Once you have centered a grapefruit-size ball of clay, open it and pull a basic cylinder. Then, while it is still spinning on the wheel, close the top rim by gradually pressing inward on both sides of the open cylinder with your fingers [4-5]. The clay will thicken and tend to ripple if you move too quickly, so take your time. You can support the top with one finger on the inside of the closing circle of clay as you stretch the outer surface toward the axis point in the middle.

To completely close the form, slip your supporting finger out of the inside cavity and press inward from the shoulder of the pot with a metal or wooden rib (a flat, smooth piece of ruler works well) until the top hole is fully covered with clay, trapping air inside like a balloon.

Once you have closed the cylinder completely, the trapped air will serve as inner support for whatever you might do to the exterior surface. If you let it stiffen a little bit, you can roll this form on rocks or sticks, paddle it into a square, and otherwise play with the shape [4-6]. You can also slice off pieces to give it angular facets.

One final note before it is finished: you must prick the surface to let the trapped air escape, or this form will crack as the clay shrinks in drying.

4-6

Variation: Closed Form with Open Base

You can make wonderful hanging planters this way.

After centering the clay, open it *all the way to the wheel head.* Leave nothing for the bottom of a pot. Then pull a cylinder and begin to collar the rim in with your hands.

Before you close the form, go back to the inside bottom rim where it meets the wheel head and clean up extra clay or water that has collected there. You will save yourself lots of time and effort if you cut away the ragged edge of clay with a wooden tool before you close up the top.

Once the form is closed (as described above), the trapped air will support considerable downward and inward pressure applied to the outside surface of the pot. You can make ridges, knobs, and a long pointed extension, if you want to [4-7].

When the form is stiff enough to hold its shape, cut it off the wheel and invert it—as a hanging planter. If you have made a fancy "bottom" that is not at all flat, you will need to put the piece in a holder so you can cut or sand the rim smooth. I

4-7

have found that unfired clay pots from the garden store work very well for this. You can buy them in any size.

Once you have finished the rim, remember to pierce three holes just below it with a knitting needle or sharp knife. The holes should be equidistant from each other for good balance.

To hang the planter after it has been fired, use a 24-inch piece of leather lacing or woven cord. (Although leather is pleasing and natural, watering plants will eventually rot the leather thong, so a woven cord is probably a better choice.) Run each end through a hole in the planter and knot it on the outside, making a loop that is anchored at both ends. Then take another 24-inch length and run it through the third hole, knotting it on the outside too. With the free end, create a slipknot to join this longer strand with the loop created by the first piece.

THROWING OFF THE HUMP

While visiting the northern part of Thailand, I had the chance to visit a production pottery and watch generations of craftspeople practice their skills. I was entranced by watching a father and son work together with a simple wooden wheel set on a shaft in the ground. The boy steadied himself with a hanging strap—like the handholds on a bus—and turned the wheel steadily with one bare foot, while his father shaped many small bowls, one after the other, on the top of a large mound of clay on the wheel. When one bowl had been quickly shaped, the father cut it off the hunk of clay and handed it to the boy's free hand while the father began another. Still hanging onto the strap with one hand, the boy would give the wheel a quick spin and pivot on his planted foot to deposit the bowl on a long board that was filled with the father's handiwork. They kept up a lively stream of talk all the while, and the boy seemed to be amused by my interest.

This technique of using the top part of a larger lump of clay on the wheel is called "throwing off the hump" and is most useful for making many small pieces. You only have to center the small piece at the top that you will be working on, letting the little bit of water that you add for shaping soften the clay immediately below where you are working.

I once had an order for a hundred small Communion cups that did not have to be identical, but needed to look as though they belonged to a family. It was the perfect occasion for throwing them off the hump—and I remembered the Thai father and son as I saw my little porcelain cups lined up on long boards in my own studio. Whenever there is a need for some uniformity (I think of it as familiarity), throwing off the hump is an easy way to fall into a rhythm that shows in the dance of shaping clay on a potter's wheel.

Variation: Throwing a Lid

If you want to make a project with a lid (such as a cookie jar), making the body and the lid from the same piece of clay will ensure that both pieces have equal wetness, so the lid won't shrink more than the pot or vice versa. This is where "throwing off the hump" works especially well.

Start by kneading the whole piece of clay (I usually use 8 to 10 pounds), and plop it firmly onto the wheel. Then center only what you need for the lid. (That means you won't be adding a lot of water to center the whole mass.)

Then throw the lid like a small bowl, paying particular attention to flattening the rim, because that will need to sit firmly on the "shelf" inside the neck of the pot. When the "bowl" is finished, squeeze the clay below the bowl to create a thick stump, which you will later throw as a knob. (Usually the "stump" is thick enough that it will stay pretty moist.) Then cut the lid off the hump, set it aside to dry, and continue throwing the body of the pot. Set the finished body aside.

4-8

When the rim of the lid is leather-hard, turn the lid over and center it on the wheel. You must secure the lid to the wheel by sticking it on with three balls of clay. Use a fettling (thin-bladed) knife to cut a hole in the center, down through the stump and into the inner space of the lid. That's where your inner finger will work as you begin to throw a tiny cylinder with your fingers.

Be careful not to twist the knob off the lid as you throw. Once a cylinder is formed, you can close it and use the trapped air to support whatever round shape you might want to create [4-8].

5
Finishing
Trimming Away the Excess

There is a time
to leave behind
what isn't needed
to stand alone in the world.

There is no outside authority to tell me when a pot is finished—no standard or rule except my desire to explore the full potential of each piece of clay. I wait for a sense of completion, a certain knowing that I have done what I can, and then I stop. I have to *care enough* to quit, to let go of one thing for the next, to trust that more will come.

The question of final shape is some combination of need and skill. The purpose for making any particular form will, in many ways, guide the way a piece is finished. If a tea bowl or cup is to be used for drinking, you will want to have a smooth lip that is not too sharp and yet not too thick. Pitchers must pour, spouts should not drip, handles need to be holdable, and lids should fit. If a decorative piece will be placed on a table or shelf, smoothing the bottom rim so it won't scratch the furniture is important. If the pot will be used outside as a planter, you need to think about drainage.

Aesthetic questions arise as well. In our day, nobody really "needs" handmade pottery anymore. Factories produce plates and cups and bowls that are functional and well designed. But there is something so intrinsically satisfying about the dimensional quality of handmade pottery that I believe we know when something is "right" by feel and intuition.

Finishing a pot is the time to step back and let the resonance between potter and clay become clear. It's a step beyond intention, beyond skill and experience. I've seen soulless pots that were thrown with great precision, and beginning efforts fairly bursting with life. Sometimes people fuss over the finishing touches and drain away the vitality that was there in the original form. My advice to potters is simple: "Work carefully until it feels finished, and then stop."

Each ending is a little death, closing off the possibility of further change. When I begin the trimming process and focus on the finishing touches—a strong foot, a definitive rim, the particular line of the whole shape—the spell of my creative energy is broken. The finishing step takes care, attention, and release. Finishing is an act of faith in the principle of renewal, which stands against my fear that nothing more will come. Choosing to end a creative process means letting go of some things, no matter how important they are, to make space for the new. Finishing also means trusting that something in us—our spiritual source—is forever being creative, always wanting to give birth. *Eros* is always there in the wings.

The rhythm of start and finish, of trimming away the excess clay around the bottom because it is no longer needed to support a soft and changing wall, is as common as breathing in and breathing out. Our bodies do it all the time: breathe out the past and breathe in the future. But being conscious of the transition moments when we stand poised between past and future takes courage and practice.

CARVING

After shaping the pot with my hands inside and out, I use a wooden tool to carve away extra thickness that has been left around the base for support. This extra "tail" of clay is not wasted—it will be kneaded into the next day's work—but for now, it is no longer needed. To leave it would make the pot seem heavy and awkward, unskillfully made. To remove it is part of reaching for congruence between the inner shape and the outer form. Only the potter knows how much must be left for stability.

Peeling away a base of support when we do not need it anymore, or when we are moving on to something new, is a lifetime process of relinquishment. Each time we move from one place to another, we pare down our possessions, leave things behind. We may promise that close friendships will continue, but not all do. We leave familiar schools and neighborhoods and jobs, imagining that the Internet will keep us close, but at some level we know that long-distance friendship won't ever be the same as sharing space in person. We may leave our friends with a sense of dread, wondering whether we'll ever find new friends as close. Our culture suggests we can have it all—mobility and permanence, autonomy and community. Parents who keep our sentimental favorites may serve as a kind of insurance against rootlessness—or we may haul the stuff around with us in unopened boxes. Giving up the "family home" becomes difficult for adult children because we have often stored our early treasures (yearbooks, scrapbooks, favorite clothes) with parents until they move to a retirement place.

Carving away these external supports can help make us aware of our inner lives, but it can also leave us feeling lonely and bereft. As each generation becomes more mobile or transient, the human fabric of soul and community is stretched thinner and thinner. But if we trust that each new shape of our lives will have the support it needs, that each ending gives birth to another beginning, then we can finish a particular piece (or work or call) with confidence ... or at least with enough courage to do it.

After my father died, I watched my mother move from our family home to a small "independent living" apartment. She chose what she wanted to keep and let us, her daughters, dispose of the rest. She made new friends there—people who shared her interests and energy level. Then, after a decade, she moved again to be near my younger sister, leaving behind that circle of friends for a new state and a smaller apartment, with more help. At eighty-seven, she seemed remarkably resilient—and lucky to find a special friend across the hall, along with a table of stimulating men and women to share meals with. At the end of her life, she moved once again, into a single room for "assisted living." By then, her circle of support was pared down to a few special things (artwork, chair, lamp, and books), a paid companion, and the daily attention of her daughters. Each time she moved, a truer shape of her soul was revealed. Her death at ninety-one seemed a final release of her body/home; it was no longer needed.

Japanese potters have a saying: "The true shape of a pot is what is left when the jar is broken." Learning to let go of what we do not need for the present situation is a lifelong process.

When I think of carving away the excess clay at the foot of a pot, I think of how it enhances the whole shape. A narrow foot provides contrast so I can see more clearly the subtle lines of neck, shoulder, and belly. A wide foot can give stability to a cup or pitcher. And when we carve away external supports in our lives that are no longer needed, we, too, can better see the true shape of our souls.

Letting Go

- Close your eyes and imagine yourself walking slowly through your house or apartment. Stop and notice the things that feel most important, that you would want to take with you if you were moving to a smaller living space. Ask yourself what those things symbolize for you, for your soul.

- Then, if you can, find a picture of yourself twenty years ago, and study the picture. How have you changed? What have you started and finished during those years? Write about those changes and what they mean to you.

- Finally, focus on something you have let go of recently, something that you once needed for support. How do you feel about letting go of that (house, job, relationship, clothing, books)?

TRIMMING

Once the pot is cut off the wheel, it is inverted and left to dry. When the bottom is leather-hard, I take a metal cutting tool and trim away even more. Congruence is once again important, not only because a bottom that is left too thick can pull into an S-crack during the final drying or firing, but also because I want the look and feel of a pot to match. Trimming a pot marks the shift from something I am making for myself to consciousness of how others might react to it. Mentally, I step away from my creation and look at it as an observer, a silent witness.

The foot of a pot literally gives it something to stand on.

Trimming lifts the body from a table surface, so light can get under it and shade the contour for better visual definition. Every potter has a characteristic way of "footing" a bowl. Some like it rough, and others, smooth. Some like a plain foot that contrasts with the glaze to be applied later; others finish the foot with its own coat of slip, a liquid clay that can be colored but does not run like glaze. My pots generally have a pronounced pedestal foot, which is brushed with an iron band marking the edge of the glaze coating and defining the clean, smooth, bare rim. The way I foot my bowls gives them a classic form. Others in this postmodern

Footed bowl by Louie Mideke.

95

age purposely flaunt conventional notions of beauty and let their pots stand as thrown.

The pots that I build by hand are harder to trim because they are usually asymmetrical. Pinched or coiled pots take longer, are more individual, and are more likely to be ritual pots commemorating some significant event. I rarely put a distinctive foot on my hand-built pots. They seem, rather, to grow out of the supporting surface, like a root out of dry ground. Those pots are still connected to the earth, like a dream or half-formed sentence. They have no distinct beginning because the clay does not have to be centered and opened, nor do they have a distinct foot to end with. Nevertheless, these pots, like all the others, must be trimmed and smoothed for whatever function they have in the world.

In life, rituals are something like the foot of a bowl: they help us complete events and move on; they bring closure. They remind us that we belong to something larger—a family, tribe, community of people, and a story that is longer than our lives.

Not long ago, a friend of mine from the Seekers community died suddenly, and her husband wanted a larger pot to hold her ashes for a lakeside ceremony, and a smaller pot for him to keep some of her ashes at home. Since they loved to dance and had been skilled tango partners, I put on some tango music while I worked and let the music guide my fingers in long sweeping movements. A narrow base, like dancing feet in tandem, seemed appropriate. And when the pots were dry, I smoothed them with sandpaper and colored them with pastel chalk, giving each the "feel" of my friend's delicate grace and lively humor. The larger one went into the lake with her ashes, dissolving into mud again. The smaller one remains a memento, a secure and yet fragile unfired clay container—a reminder of how fleeting life can be.

There is no right or wrong way to foot a bowl—or to ritualize events in our lives. But because we have largely lost a sense of having a sacred community, many of us have lost a community with whom we can celebrate traditional rites of passage: puberty, marriage, baptism, retirement, death. Secular rituals, such as getting a driver's license or having an elaborate wedding at a local hotel, do not have the spiritual power because they are not grounded in a story that is larger than the individuals involved.

Without a community of family or friends, or church or synagogue for a larger context, it is hard to "foot the bowl" of our lives. Sometimes we need to create a temporary community around an event. When my mother died, it seemed important to have an immediate memorial service so the friends and staff members of her assisted-living facility could say "farewell" to her and move on with their lives. The chaplain of the facility urged us to have a service in the chapel, which was in another building. My sister and I argued instead for a small room in my mother's building, so that friends in wheelchairs and staff members on duty could attend. The chaplain reluctantly agreed, saying, "It's never been done that way before." But when the room was filled with people who had been my mother's community in her last days, he acknowledged how helpful it was for all of them. Several months later, we had a more formal memorial service in the church where my mother had spent most of her life, for her extended family and those longtime friends who were still alive. The first service was a "quick trim," and the second, "footing the bowl" of her life.

I thought of my mother's dream during the last week of her life, where she had seen herself crawling in a line of women toward an opening in the veil of mystery. When I had asked her if she knew any of the women, she had said, "No, but we've all been called to go." To me, that is the essence of our soul's path. As children, we bond with our parents and cling to favorite things. As we mature, we learn that nothing is permanent, but that there are stories and rituals to sustain us as we respond to the deep pulse of call to be truly human and to feel our connection with all parts of creation on the journey of the soul.

Rites of Passage

- Describe a ceremonial ritual that has helped you make a major life transition. What elements were particularly important? Were there elements of the ritual that made the transition easier? Harder?

- Do you have a sacred community with whom you can celebrate transitions? If so, what community rituals mean the most to you? If not, is a sacred community something that is important for you to find or develop?

CLAIMING

Once I have formed the foot and smoothed the bottom rim of a pot, I cover the area inside the rim with a layer of slip and sign my name through the thin coat of color, into the body itself. Like the ancient artists in the Neolithic caves of Europe and Africa who signed their work with handprints, I, too, am putting my mark on my work. My signature acknowledges this pot as one of mine. But signing my work does more than put my stamp on it; it implies that I believe a community will care about and receive what I am offering.

As I write my name in the soft clay, I am aware of some risk and a sense of exposure. I imagine others looking at this piece, judging it perhaps with critical eyes, so the choice to scribe my name or initials into the clay takes a little courage. I am willing to be responsible for what I make. With my signature, this pot becomes part of my legacy to others. I remember, with some chagrin, the first time I saw one at a yard sale. Then I realized that no legacy is ever permanent.

Claiming my work this way could be seen as a sign of wanting to "mark my territory," but I see it as an invitation to dialogue and interaction. I like to know where my pots go, to establish a conversation with the new owners. I want to know who is receiving them, to feel the extended community of celebration around handmade things. Perfectionists can purchase goods made by machine, all alike. I prefer the messiness of real people in direct contact—a school for our souls.

It seems to me that having a community to receive our gifts is an important piece of the creative process. Attentive parents try to give that to their children, to let them know that others care about what they do, how they act, and what they create. But as we grow up and realize that others really do not care as much about our special gifts, we tend to put them away and do only what we get paid for. The secret is that joy and creativity thrive where our gifts are given freely, without counting the cost, often in the long and unpaid hours we spend with dear friends and family. In my own life, a secret joy has been making baby quilts for each of my nieces and nephews, and now their children. Nobody could pay me enough to make those quilts for sale.

But what if nobody wanted the gifts of time, energy, and creativity that I bring? What happens to our creativity when there is no community to receive what we have to offer?

The good news is that we each have the power to reach out to others and begin to create that kind of community. No matter where we live or work, every person has the power to ask for help or to offer kindness and attention, which are the seeds of community. It can begin with a quilting circle, or a scrapbooking session, or a clay class at the local craft center. I believe that handwork may be the seed of a new community wherever we find ourselves.

Making It Yours

- How do you sign your name to things that you have made? Or *do* you?

- What is the story of your name? What would be your descriptive tagline or nickname?

- Do you have a business card? What does it say about you? If you were to design a soulcard, what would it say? How might it look?

• Have you experienced a community that cared about
your creativity? Do you have one now? Is there
something you would like to learn or give that could
develop such a community?

COMPLETION

Finishing something requires that we have the whole picture in
mind. Completion also requires care and attention to detail, even if
we might rather be starting another creation. After a pot is trimmed
and signed, it is time to add a handle or a spout or some other decorative touch out of clay. Although the clay is stiff and damp, it is
still fragile and must be handled with care. If the clay has gotten too
dry, these appendages will not adhere properly and will tend to
crack off during the drying process. If the clay is too wet, the wall of
the pot will not support the weight of an added spout or handle.

In the Southwest, where natural clay tends to be unsuitable for
throwing on a wheel, completion involves sanding and burnishing
the clay to a fine sheen. After coiling and paddling a pot, sanding it
with a fine-mesh screen and fine-gauge sandpaper will leave the surface smooth and ready for further decoration. Burnishing, best done
with a very smooth stone or the back of a silver spoon, requires careful attention because the leather-hard clay is still damp and a thin
wall can easily be broken when the pressure of burnishing is applied.

Finishing something important is never easy. It requires inten-
tionality and tolerance for loss. Wholeness can be broken. Risk is
always part of completion. Yet creativity must have a stopping
point, or it becomes cancerous. Caring enough to stop making
adjustments is one way of treating endings as a normal part of the
life process, which we can do if we believe new life will come again.
By giving special attention to the ending as well as the beginning,
we learn the principle of ebb and flow. Nothing is meant to be permanent, even the stone that clay first came from. Finishing is both
an act of trust and an act of faith in the nature of the universe.

After two decades as the editor and publisher of the *Faith at Work* magazine, it felt as if I were coming to the end of my work there. I had already relinquished my role as president of the organization, and I could see the need for a shift in the magazine that would appeal more to a younger generation. It would take me two more years to accomplish the handoff to a new editor, but at the close, I felt satisfied that the magazine had been trimmed and footed with as much integrity as I could give it.

In the months after my final issue of the magazine, I left my coat at a restaurant, lost my purse, misplaced my keys, and forgot appointments. Everything pointed toward inner distress and distraction. My dreams were no help. I felt stuck at the crossroads between my old work and whatever new was coming. Then a friend suggested that we could set up a dialogue with the Seekers community to explore my understanding of call. She lined up the date, sent me her questions, and invited me into prayerful preparation. When the day came, I was a nervous wreck. I felt vulnerable and inadequate. I realize now that my soul was not sure that she would appear at the party.

Parker Palmer, the Quaker teacher and writer, has written extensively about the soul as a "wild animal," usually shy and skittish in public settings. That's exactly what I was feeling—that my soul might not show her face at this gathering. But I realized it was important for me to see my vocational call to Faith at Work come to completion within a larger faith context. I don't think it was an accident that the lectionary text for that Sunday happened to be about the temptations of Jesus. The three temptations helped me put my story in perspective. I saw the first temptation—to turn stones into bread—as a temptation to solve problems, to use my intellectual skills to find a solution rather than trusting my gut, especially when the risks had seemed overwhelming.

I saw the second temptation—to worship worldly success—as something that had been tempered all along by my reluctance to "institutionalize" Faith at Work. Maybe worldly success had never been much of a temptation for me. Since its inception, Faith at

Work had always been essentially a relational movement, with personal storytelling at its heart, and it simply did not fit with the model of efficiency and mass production.

Finally, I understood that the third temptation—to reach for immortality—was at the heart of my desire to retain control of the magazine. Although my soul knew it was time to move on, my ego-self wanted to keep things as they were.

There was something very powerful about exposing that pretension in front of our little congregation. My church community had walked with me, celebrated with me, and was now helping me let go. Without my community, I doubt that I could have released the piece of my identity that was tied up in Faith at Work. I would probably still be grieving.

In her poem "In Blackwater Woods," Mary Oliver speaks to the importance of completing whatever soulwork we have been given to do in this life. She names three things that are essential to living. The first essential thing, to love what is mortal, challenges the reader to love what will surely die, broadening the object of our loving embrace to all living things. In effect, this is a thread that runs throughout this book and is a core meaning of soulwork. Oliver goes on to say that our lives depend on being able to "hold it against [our] bones." In other words, our lives depend on learning how to love deeply and fully. The final line of the poem states beautifully, and boldly, that our final task is to let go "when the time comes to let it go." Yes. This is the discipline of soulwork that we can practice over and over with clay.

Try It with Clay!

SANDING AND SCRAPING

If you are planning to burnish a pot, sanding or scraping the pot will smooth out tiny ridges and make the burnishing more successful. Use a very fine-grit sandpaper or the edge of a jar lid, if that fits the curve of your pot. Sanding is rarely necessary on a thrown pot, except where trimming has left a rough or grainy surface that you do not want. The decision about whether to sand a pot or a sculpture really depends on your vision for the finished surface. I usually sand the bottom rim of my pots, especially if they won't be fired, so they will not mar the surface of a shelf or table.

BURNISHING WITH OIL

For many years, I thought that the only way to burnish was to work on leather-hard clay, but then I discovered that you can soften the surface of a bone-dry pot with vegetable oil or baby oil (one section at a time) and burnish it successfully. Remember that bone-dry clay is more fragile than leather-hard clay, so you will have to be very careful when putting the pressure of burnishing on the wall of the pot. You *must* support the inner surface with your fingers or a stone while burnishing the outer surface.

PULLING A HANDLE

Almost every person who works with clay wants to experiment with making a mug. And once you move beyond a tea bowl, that requires making a handle. The main thing to remember is that the handle is a separate piece of clay, of different wetness, and therefore a different rate of shrinkage.

For a mug, I like to "pull a handle" from the same clay body that the mug is made from. This will take some practice. Begin by kneading a fist-size ball of clay and rolling it into a slightly elongated shape. Then, holding it up in one hand, begin pulling it downward between the thumb and forefinger of your other hand, squeezing firmly and evenly [5-1]. The action is like milking a cow. You will need to use plenty of water to keep the rope of clay from breaking off.

When you have 4 or 5 inches of clay extended, you can turn the lump of clay in your holding hand so the handle curves with its own weight [5-2]. I usually let the handle rest against that lump of handheld clay until it stiffens enough to hold that shape. Then it can be attached to the cup by roughening two places on the cup where you want to attach the handle. Roughen the top surface of the handle as well and attach that first, pressing and smoothing the joint. Then attach the bottom of the handle so the curve is maintained [5-3].

Once you have mastered pulling a handle, such "ribbons" of clay can be used on the top of a casserole, down the sides of a vase, or in any other decorative way that you choose. Once again, the size and style of any handle should fit with the overall design and function of your piece. But don't forget to be playful. Experiment. Ask yourself, "What if I did this ... or that?"

5-1

5-2

A Spout That Pours

Making a small pitcher for syrup or cream can also be fun. If you have pinched or thrown a small cylinder (it does not need to have a handle), wait until it is on the wet side of leather-hard because you will be stretching the rim itself to make a pouring spout.

Place your thumb and forefinger on the outside of the rim to support the wall of the pot. Then, using plenty of water, use the index finger of your other hand and stroke the clay outward to make a spout. To widen the pouring area, you can also move your finger side to side—but don't make it too wide. The clay will thin where you are stretching it, and that will break the stream of liquid when used for pouring. But you also don't want to make it too thin, or it will crack there. Be careful not to deform the rest of the pot as you are making the spout. (This motion can also be used for a teapot spout that has been thrown on the wheel and attached like a handle.) This pitcher [5-4] by Louie Mideke makes the pouring spout into a humorous beaked bird (notice where he put the eyes!).

5-3

There is nothing more annoying than a teapot that drips or doesn't pour well. If you find that a pouring spout does dribble after it has been glazed and fired, put a little bit of epoxy sealant on the underside of the lip to break the pouring stream.

SEAT FOR A LID

When I am making a burial urn for someone's ashes, I want to make sure that the lid fits securely. I usually start with about 8 pounds of clay on the wheel and throw the lid off the hump first. Then I measure the diameter of the lid with calipers, planning to leave the neck of the pot a little thicker than I would when making a pot without a lid. When the basic cookie-jar shape is completed,

5-4

5-5

I take a ruler or some other right-angled piece of wood and, supporting the wall just under the top rim with the fingers of my left hand, press straight down with the ruler on the inside of the rim to make a "seat" for the lid [5-5].

The motion of pressing downward will thicken the clay just under the ruler's edge, making a clear shelf of clay for the lid to rest on. I like to make the seat deep enough so the width of the lid sits securely on that shelf. Once that is done, you can make minor adjustments in the neck of the pot to make a good fit between the seat and the lid [5-6].

A ROLLED FOOT

5-6

If you want a round shape to stand upright instead of rolling over on its side, you will have to think about its foot. The simplest way of creating a foot is, of course, to tap a rounded bottom on a tabletop to flatten one spot. Or use the slightly rounded back of a wooden spoon to make a small indentation in the middle of the bottom so there will be a single ring of clay on which to stand.

If you have a cylinder of clay and you want a slight indentation in the middle of the flat foot, roll the outside of the base on a flat surface; the compression will cause a slight lift in the softer center of the foot.

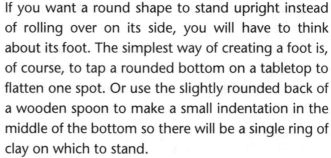

SLAB BUILDING

Building large pieces with slabs of clay is fast and easy, but finishing is the critical step if you want these rectilinear forms to survive their firing.

Slabs can be made by slapping the clay between your hands, or by slapping it down on a hard surface and stretching it out like pizza dough. Slabs can also be rolled out with a rolling pin or pressed out with a mechanical slab roller.

5-7

Because the clay is quite damp (like cookie dough) when making a slab, it should be set on a table on top of a piece of canvas or target cloth (unbleached muslin, which can be purchased by the roll at most fabric stores) to facilitate drying on both sides. While supported by this hard surface, slabs may be cut into shapes and textured with fingers, stamps, or a rolled pattern [5-7].

5-8

If you are new to slab building, I recommend that you start by making a tall cylinder from one slab of clay. When the clay has stiffened a little, cut a round piece (like a cookie) for the bottom of the cylinder and make sure the slab has a cut side that equals the circumference of the circle plus a little. Raise the textured slab and place it around the clay "cookie," pressing a coil of clay into the bottom seam on the inside before you close the side seam with another coil.

You may need to support the cylinder [5-8] with a cardboard cylinder from a roll of paper towels until it stiffens sufficiently to stand alone. When you can handle the cylinder without deforming it, make sure that the seam around the bottom is pressed in tightly [5-9]. I like to roll the bottom of the cylinder on a hard surface

5-9

5-10

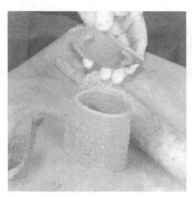

5-11

5-12

to create a slight rim and compress the seam at the same time. Be sure to remove the inner support before the clay shrinks too tightly around it.

BOX WITH A LID

To make a box from several slabs of clay, make sure you start with slabs that are the same thickness and wetness. You can use something as simple as a cereal box as a template for cutting a rectangular pattern in each slab. Texture the pieces while they are still flat, and then assemble the box by placing the walls on edge around the base of the box. Join the inside corners with coils of clay so you don't spoil the texture on the outside. You can also make a round "box" [5-10] by using a single slab of clay.

You can cut your lid either to fit down into the box or to rest on top [5-11]. To fit down inside, cut the lid to match the base of your box. You can make a seat for it by affixing a coil—roughed and pressed—around the top inside of the box. If you want your lid to sit on top, cut it slightly larger than the base. You can make an anchor for this style of lid by pressing a coil into the underside of the lid so the coil fits down into the cavity of the box and holds the lid in place.

Slab-built forms are usually rectilinear, so you might finish this box with an angular knob, made by forming two square beads of clay and cutting a small strip of clay to be joined to the lid with a little slip. The knob can be added while the pieces are still flat on the table for support [5-12].

DRAPE MOLD

Slabs can also be used to create beautiful soft curves with the help of what is called a "drape mold." These smooth plaster molds are sold by craft suppliers, but you can use any rounded shape for a single curved container: a soccer ball, a beach ball, even a cloth stretched between the four corners of a box.

On a piece of canvas or pastry cloth, roll out a slab of clay, and then cut the shape you want with a needle or fettling (thin-bladed) knife. It will be like working with pie dough, so you must lift it carefully, using the canvas to hold it together to keep the clay from tearing.

If you are using a ball for your mold, cover your slab with another piece of cloth, and then roll or tip it onto the ball so the second cloth is lying against the ball. (This will keep it from sticking to the plastic and help you remove it later.) Secure the ball to keep it from rolling around, then pull the canvas away from the slab to let it stiffen.

Instead of using just one slab, you can use several strips to make a bowl, as shown here [5-13].

Once the slab is fairly stable, I like to add a foot of some kind by rolling out a snake of clay and attaching it to the bottom of the slab while the ball continues to offer support. (You may need to experiment with the size of the foot a little. If the foot is too small for the slab's extension, there is always the danger of slumping during firing. Experimentation will be your best guide.)

5-13

Finally, when the foot is dry enough to support the weight of the slab, you'll need to have some kind of support ready for the underside of the rim before you turn the draped slab over. You could use a rolled towel or cardboard tubes from rolls of paper towels, if they are the right size. Before you flip your project over, if you are going to texture the outside surface in any way, this is the time to do it.

Once the slab is fully dry, it should be able to hold the curve that your drape mold has created. Gently flip the dried clay over onto your supports. Then you can add further texture to the inside, if you wish.

Variation: Two-Sided Drape Mold

You can make a stunning lamp base or a large vase by using two slabs instead of one. You will need two identical drape molds. Something with a large surface, such as a beach ball, works well. Some people use two small garbage cans with a piece of knit jersey stretched over each one as the drape mold, and then they use the lid as a circular pattern.

Roll out two slabs and cut them with the same pattern. Press each one into a sling or onto a ball as described above. At the same time, pat out a pancake for the base from the same clay. When all three pieces have stiffened enough to hold their shape, use bunched-up newspaper to hold the inside cavity as you join one curved slab to the other (the newspaper will burn out during firing, so you can leave it there). Before joining the two sides together, roughen each surface. Then wet the seam with a slurry of clay and reinforce it with a coil of clay pressed firmly into the seam.

The next step is to add the base. Use a fettling knife to cut away some clay at the bottom of each side and attach the base in the same way that you attached the sides. Because you are making a closed form, with air and newspaper inside, if you stand the closed form on its base, the weight of the pot will help seal that joint, and you can work on the joining seam, smoothing it some more.

The final step is to open a hole at the top so that moisture can escape. If this is going to be a lamp base, make sure the opening fits the hardware that you will be inserting to wire the lamp. You will also need to make a hole at the bottom for the cord.

A rounded shape like this can be asymmetrical and very sensu-ous. I have seen beautiful lamp bases made this way by using a high bisque firing and then doing a quick smoke fire in a garbage can with sawdust or newspaper to create "clouds" of smoky color.

6
Decorating
Adding a Playful Touch

A splash here,
a line there,
add interest and color
to the plain surface.

Why does the potter decorate a pot at all? Why not leave the clay as it is? The answer is as old as humankind: we are created with the capacity for play and imagination. We want to do something with a plain surface. The impulse for color and texture seems to be ingrained, while uniformity feels oppressive. In the natural world, diversity reigns and uneven patterns abound.

Decoration as the capacity for play takes us back to the dawn of creation and to the very nature of God. Beyond human life, before animals and plants, to the sheer variety of basic elements and combinations that make up the network of life on earth, we have a sense of experimentation, of abundance and pleasure in variety. "What if ..." and "Why not ..." become a field for development and diversity.

Humans are not confined to living with what we have and what we know. We can envision the future as something different from the present and take steps to achieve it. Even if we do not name ourselves as artists, we all have the capacity for vision and creativity. We can risk and learn from what does not work because we are created to be creators. The source of creation is within.

If we can move beyond "like" and "dislike," and embrace both the intentional experiments and accidents of creativity, we are feeding the soul with delight and possibility. This stance is the opposite of production and product, goal setting and accomplishment. The Sufi poet Rumi writes of this state: "There is a field beyond right and wrong. I'll meet you there."

TEXTURING

All over the world, humans use clay because it is soft enough to mold, and yet hardens into semipermanence with fire. Adding texture to the surface of a thrown pot probably began with noticing the marks that animal feet made in clay next to a stream. As early humans began to make little figurines, to scratch lunar cycle records into soft clay, or to make handprints on cave walls, they also discovered the simple delight in decoration. Pinching or twisting the clay created vinelike patterns, and soon a recognizable iconography of symbols developed in different bioregions. Forest dwellers incised plant shapes that were their main food source, and plains dwellers featured the animals they hunted. Circular symbols for unity and spiral images for the passage of time were common for these hunter-gatherer people.

Smooth or rough, thin or thick, clay is both malleable to the touch and able to retain the shape once an object or a hand is removed. When a pot has been thrown on a wheel, it is difficult to eliminate the spiral left by the inner and outer pressure of the potter's fingers. Those ridges are a sign of authenticity and authorship. They tell the viewer that this was not poured into a mold or made by a machine. Further texturing often complements the horizontal rings left by the potter. Any hard surface can be used to imprint clay: stone, wood, glass, kitchen utensils, hardware, rope, keys, woodblocks, or rolling dies. In addition, some potters paddle the pot to flatten or otherwise change its shape. Ancient Incas and Persians of about the same time made elaborate repetitive patterns using carved rollers. Some artists add color and texture with clay slips or engobes (more elaborately constructed slips) that have been prepared beforehand. At the decorative point in the process, there are many options and few restrictions.

When I first began making pots, I was afraid to alter the shape of my pots too much for fear that they would collapse. Now, I trust the creative process enough to be curious about those accidents and see them as part of the larger revelation that is taking place, literally, beneath my hands. There are no rules, except what the materials will and won't do.

Each of us leaves our "mark" on the life we live, on the work we do, on the relationships we have. As I look back on my years at Faith at Work, I can see many textures that marked the work as mine. I can also see how my work expanded as I was able to trust the creative process. One of my core projects was to develop a series of retreat designs based on biblical stories. Each one followed a basic framework for a weekend event, but each one was different because each event was team-led, not dependent upon an expert leader. This made room for the contributions of a variety of leaders who "decorated" the basic structure with individual energies and ideas. Each event became a separate creation, not something that could be copyrighted and marketed. And because I was interested in empowering people to understand the process as well as the content, each event became a learning opportunity for everyone involved. I suspect that this methodology flowed from my experience in Louie Mideke's pottery studio, where I learned by *doing* as much as by reading and watching him work.

My new work now, of making unfired burial urns, calls for a different kind of imprint. These urns need to be attractive enough for a formal memorial service, yet temporary enough to dissolve in water or the ground. I am finding that simple surface decoration—carving through a slip or distressing the surface with my hands—feels appropriate. I let the shape of each pot suggest its decoration.

On a recent trip to the Grand Canyon, I found a beautiful wooden weaver's tool for tamping the wool on a backstrap loom. It reminded me of a bear's claw, and I have been using it for scratching the surface of some urns. (For a picture of the results of this technique, see the photos on page 106.) On others, I've embedded a special stone or plant imprint. Symbols and objects from nature speak of the larger story of ongoing creation that we are living even as we die: *ashes to ashes, dust to dust.*

Leaving a mark can also be a sign of blessing and stewardship. When our Seekers church moved into a new space—a century-old house we had renovated—everyone was invited to make a 4-inch tile so we could install one in each room as it was blessed for our use. Some people used precast greenware tiles, some made them by hand. Some used paper, others painted on wood, and several made mosaics of broken and glued china. Each tile was put in a plexiglass box to protect it and fix it to the wall in an inconspicuous place. Now each room, including the bathrooms, has a sign of blessing from the ritual we created as we claimed each room for our use. We view this old house as part of God's larger story of hospitality for all, and these handmade tiles acknowledge our part of that vision.

The Texture of Your Life

- The texture of your life is conveyed in many ways—by speech, manner, and clothing. What kind of clothing are you wearing right now? What can you tell from the different textures that you are wearing? How does your clothing reflect what you imagined for your day?

- What colors and textures are you most drawn to in nature? What examples of those favorite colors or textures do you have in your home? What do they say about you and your style of life?

- If you were to create a clay tile to install in a special place, what would it look like? Where might you place it?

GLAZING

If shaping and texturing a pot means concentrating on the present moment, then glazing gives it a promised future. A potter is forced to project forward in time because she is working with ground stone, not organic colorants, and these natural minerals will change radically with heat in a kiln. Chromium pink turns bright green; copper gray turns red; and dull iron browns can have a deep rust glow or a brilliant crimson sparkle, depending on the temperature and time allowed for firing.

Learning the chemistry of glaze construction was a surprising doorway into the natural world that I had not expected. It provided me with a laboratory experience where spirituality and science could meet with a mystery akin to medieval alchemy. Mixing glazes can be as simple as preparing a clay slip from one source or as complex as a lab chemist attempting to reproduce something in nature. More than any other part of the process, glazing involves choice and imagination.

My pottery teacher, Louie, had studied pictures and collected examples of classic Japanese and Chinese pots, some of them more than five thousand years old. He wanted to reproduce those glazes in his studio, but there were few formulas available at that time. Instead, he had to experiment and track his results. Louie developed a method of preparing glazes that allowed him to brush the glaze onto a damp clay body, using two or three coats of a basic glaze in quick succession. He often added a wax resist on top of that, and then brushed on another coat of contrasting color to bring out the wax pattern. By single-firing his pots, the body and glaze went through the same slow firing cycle, interacting as one complete transaction. It was a risky procedure, but it gave his pots a quiet luster and depth I have rarely seen elsewhere. He knew the clay would shrink up to 15

Porcelain vase with iron splash in reduction firing.

percent in the drying process, and the time-consuming effort could simply flake off. But Louie worked hard to grind the glazes in a ball mill so they would fit the clay body, with shrinkage factored in, and he was convinced that the glaze formed a tighter bond with the clay during firing as a result. Most potters prefer to bisque fire the clay first, then dip or spray the glaze for greater speed and efficiency, but I was Louie's student and I accepted the discipline of his practice.

The risks we took were less apparent because we made them routine. Like walking a tightrope, we practiced and kept notes until we knew each glaze by its idiosyncrasies. Some shrank more than others. Some dried more quickly or tended to bond with another glaze more than to the body of the pot. Louie taught me to be observant, to make notes, and to be systematic about experimenting. At the same time, he showed me how to receive unexpected results with surprise and wonder instead of judgment. His goal was to glaze each pot to enhance its character.

From Louie, I learned patience and watchfulness. Although he read widely, he valued direct experience even more. He always started with local materials to see whether we could discover a slip or simple glaze mixed by Mother Nature. In this age when apprenticeships have largely disappeared from our culture, I realize now that this is what he offered me—apprenticeship. Although I was pretty unconscious of how rare it was to share studio space with such a skilled craftsman, I am grateful. He taught me to "love what is mortal" and "hold it against my bones" just by the way he lived his life and went about his work.

In retrospect, I see that I was learning *how to learn from experience*. By making regular notes, I learned to keep a journal. By translating those notes back into my work, I began to trust my own line of inquiry and detach from the heavy dose of academic authoritarianism that I had received in school. Because Louie was handy with tools and largely self-taught as a potter, he gave me a place where I could trust my own experience and keep growing mindfully. He watched, commented, and suggested, but never belittled my efforts to grow. Glazing with Louie not only taught me the skills needed by the artist in me, but also provided a school for my soul.

Time and effort spent glazing can be a spiritual discipline that is both demanding and beautiful. It requires knowledge, practice, and curiosity. Like Japanese brush painting, glazing can awaken our sensitivity to the natural world and stretch our imagination at the same time. Yet glazing does not need to be extensive or intricate. A bold splash of iron oxide on the shoulder of a vase may be all that it needs to be elegant. Because glazing is about enhancement rather than necessity, it would be easy to overlook this exercise of creativity as a necessity for the soul.

Just as a potter's choices for glazing enhance a pot without betraying its basic character, so, too, the choices we make about basic needs—food, clothing, shelter, and work—can either drain or nurture our souls. We can treat those things as economic factors—or as soulwork. Fresh food, grown locally and cooked lovingly with a sense of celebration, invites a special kind of community around the table. It does more than "stoke the engine" for productivity—it becomes a lens through which we can taste and touch and be in communion with the whole web of life.

Clothing, too, can enliven or deaden the soul. Like glazing, clothing can enhance or distract. It can be practical and beautiful, mass-produced in sweatshops, or purchased with care and consciousness. Although I like to dress simply and travel lightly, I buy most of my jackets at craft fairs, where I can talk with the person who made them and know that my money is supporting handwork here and abroad. When we travel to Guatemala, I look for women's cooperatives, so the money I would spend on clothes will encourage local weavers.

It's becoming obvious that fuel prices will shape our decisions about where and how to live. The size and location of our houses, accessible public transportation, and green construction will be choices that we can all make—or not. Those decisions will have not only economic ramifications, but spiritual consequences, too.

If we understand ourselves to be part of a worldwide system in which there are limited resources but nearly unlimited imagination, those choices do not need to be a terrible burden. Instead, they are simply the parameters for introducing playfulness and choice.

Like the work of glazing, soulwork requires knowledge, practice, and imagination. We have a choice to look closely at the patterns and forms of our daily lives, to engage all of our senses, to enhance our meals, rooms, and even our bodies in ways that honor the basic character of the earth and ourselves. We have the choice to exercise creativity in ways that change the promise of our future.

It's Your Choice

- How would you describe the food that you eat? What do your choices tell you about your physical connection with the land where you live?

- What is the role of decoration in your home? Your work setting?

- How would you describe your style of clothing? What does your clothing generally tell others about you?

- What kind of handwork do you do? Is there some skill that you learned directly from another person? What is it? Can you imagine doing it now as a spiritual practice?

COLOR

Breaking out of the professional potter's mold of glazing and firing happened for me by accident, literally. When I was asked to make an unfired pot to carry my friend Michael's ashes to their resting place in the Chesapeake Bay, I worried because there was no time to glaze and fire the vessel. I found that by leaving my fingerprints on the clay surface, there was enough "decoration" to make the urn seem appropriate, both solemn and festive. But there was no color beyond the natural tint of the stoneware clay itself.

Shortly after that, I took porcelain clay on a silent retreat and pinched eight small, thin bowls—one for each retreatant. As I pinched each bowl, I held that person in my mind's eye and discovered a feeling of tenderness for each one that went beyond the stories I knew about him or her. Perhaps because I was focused on the interior space of each pot, I did not really notice (or try to correct) the cracks that began to open on the exterior surface. When I finished, each pot had a smooth interior and a rough, barklike exterior. When the pots were leather-hard, I burnished the cracked exterior of each with a spoon, giving the high spots a silver-gray sheen. But the smooth interior fairly begged for a soft color. Since I also had pastels for drawing with me, I rubbed the inside of each pot with a different color. The chalky pastels seemed congruent with unfired porcelain and, as I smoothed color into the surface, the dust of the pot merged with the dust of the chalk. Almost by chance, I had discovered a very natural way to rub color onto the surface of these unfired porcelain bowls.

After that experience, I began to experiment with wet colors on damp clay, texturing through the color to reveal the white body beneath. It was a short step from that to using deep bright watercolors on dry clay, letting the wetness of the color give me a brief surface to scratch or carve through. Suddenly, I was entering a field of color.

Growing up in the Pacific Northwest, I had always been aware of the subtle variations of the green and gray of trees and water, thrilled by a crisp dawn that turned the bay into bright blue, calmed by the golden purple streaks of a late summer sunset. As I began to experiment with the immediacy of paint on clay, whether it was fired or not, I left behind the code of professional potters that would dictate the nature and content of fired glazes. A painter's palette opened up to me instead. The motion of my arm, shoulder, and body added something visceral to the experience of color for me. Not only was I adding color to the clay, but the color was alive in me as well.

I began to notice how brilliant the colors of nature are—and I stumbled across M. C. Richards's poem "Imagine Inventing Yellow." Indeed! Who could imagine the yellow of a forsythia bush? What is this miracle of color? How does a bud ripen from a curled brown nub into brash yellow branches in the spring? Or the tiny shoots of green suddenly paint the hillside with crocus purples? Or a ripe pomegranate turn lush red? Is not our love for a sunset bred deep in our genes by nature herself? Would we dream in color if we lived on the moon? What kind of creator would *think* of yellow? It's not practical. It's playful. Stimulating. Wondrous. And the urge to decorate with color comes from the same source. What does that tell us about the nature of our Creator?

Why do fresh flowers matter to me? Why does a certain color combination make me feel joyful? There's something different between the resonance that nature's color sets up in me and the intellectual appreciation I have of color in a photograph or on a digital screen. We've all seen the image of earth from space, felt wonder at the image of our blue-green world in a sea of darkness, and perhaps thought about the miracle of earth's atmosphere, along with our fears about global warming. But a picture does not evoke the same deep love that direct experience of color does.

If we are city dwellers, many of us miss the astonishing array of color and texture that contact with nature provides. The Washington, D.C., area where I live dulls my sense of color and delight—except in springtime, when the azaleas bloom everywhere. But most of the year, the formal gray marble buildings evoke stability, not drama. Grassy lawns provide a simple contrast without the riot of color that I've seen in alpine meadows or southern gardens. Through the stark grays of winter here, my soul hungers for the joy of vibrant color. I feel my heart clamp down, and I look to fire for warmth and color. There are times when I sit staring at the embers of a fire just to feel the color seep into my cells. I understand why Scandinavians, with their long, dark winters, paint their wooden toys bright red. I feel that need in my studio, painting bright colors on clay while the winds whine outside.

When I began making unfired burial urns, which are intended to dissolve with the ashes they contain, people began asking me for something that would remain with them as well. A tradition in the church has been to mark ordination with a stole, and so I began making silk prayer shawls to wear for the burial ceremony. As a sign to set apart both the ceremony and the celebrant, these painted prayer shawls have taken on a life of their own. As a contrast to the earthy colors of unfired clay, the silk stoles brim with color.

Throughout the world, indigenous people seem more responsive to nature's colors than do urban populations. Perhaps cities reflect mechanization and uniformity, while rural populations live closer to the extravagant palette of nature: colorful vegetables, flowers, and birds. In recent years, Peter and I have led a work pilgrimage for Faith at Work to the highlands of Guatemala, both to help Mayan villagers rebuild their lives after the long *violencia* in their country and to revel in the lush colors of the land and local weaving. The indigenous people, particularly the women, wear the most astonishing combinations of color and texture that I have ever seen. And that may, in fact, save their lives. Since the peace accords in 1996, the Mayas have become a tourist attraction and the government has apparently stopped its campaign of terror in favor of tourist dollars. Basic health care and education are improving in the villages, where the women retain a strong tradition of handweaving—decoration that is full of color, story, and symbols of their culture.

Alive with Color

- What colors are important to you? Look around your house, in your closet, at your dishes, and on your walls and windows, and make a list of the colors that predominate. Consider how each color makes you feel. Which color(s) would you like to see more of?

- Think of a special-occasion garment you've worn. What is the particular importance of the colors?

- Find a box of colored crayons or pastels and choose a color to describe the feeling you have about your interior life right now. Choose another for the exterior surface of your life. Notice whether they are complementary or clashing colors.

As our culture becomes more sophisticated and technological, there is a tendency to consider making things by hand as a quaint, old-fashioned way of doing things. But I think our souls yearn for expression—not by purchasing things, but by making things. Our reliance on mass-produced products has deprived us of the sheer enjoyment of using our hands and feelings and choices to shape physical materials—to say nothing of the pleasure of anticipating what the results might be, whether beautiful, useful, or unique.

According to the *Oxford English Dictionary*, the original meaning of *craft* is "strength," "force," "power," and "virtue." In German and Swedish, *kraft* moves beyond "strength" into "force of character." In Dutch, *kracht* implies "vigor" and "potency." It is only in English that there is the association of "craft" with "skill." What if we were to shift our view of "craft" from being a skill for a few to being a sign of the inner life force in each of us? What if we began to encourage the human capacity for imagination, the joy of playing with color and texture?

Perhaps we could teach crafts in the school curriculum as a basis for many other kinds of learning, about ourselves and our place in the global society. Now that we are becoming more aware of the need to preserve species diversity for the health of the planet, perhaps we could recover the joy of making things by hand, teaching one another how to do things such as cook, sew, work with wood, garden, and make things with clay.

I believe that handcrafting and decorating are not just frills—unnecessary additions to the curriculum of our lives—but fundamental to our awareness of basic forms, deep structures, and perennial patterns that could open up a new soul sensitivity in the realms of not only our personal lives, but also our cultural life and public policy.

M. C. Richards wrote in *Centering: In Pottery, Poetry and the Person*, "It is the physicality of the crafts that pleases me; I learn through my hands and my eyes and my skin what I could never learn through my brain. I develop a sense of life, of the world." I believe that the soulwork of clay can be a journey of this learning, a recovery of renewed connection with the joie de vivre, with a zest for living that encompasses our whole being. By reacquainting ourselves with the rich colors and textures of handcrafts, with the power of playful imagination, we can open new doorways to joy.

Try It with Clay!

LACEY ANGELS

When my grandmother died, I inherited a box of her handmade doilies, beautiful spidery creations made with a single crochet hook. As an immigrant from the Netherlands, she was a practical woman, cooking and canning what she grew in her garden. She sewed on her treadle sewing machine, and she spliced good apple stock onto old tree roots to experiment with local varieties of fruit during World War II. When my father went to war and my mother went to the tuberculosis sanitarium one hundred miles away, she took my sister and me in. Although she had no "spare" time, she made her doilies because the impulse to create was strong in her. Her home meant love to me, so when she died, I could not simply pass her doilies along to a consignment store, even though I could not think of how to use them.

Six years later, that box of doilies spoke to me of a new use. In my cooperative studio at the Torpedo Factory (which really had produced torpedoes during the war and then stood empty for years until a group of artists reclaimed it), the bulk of our year's income was made from October to December, and it was important to have some small items that would supplement larger sales. Angels were important to me at that time, and I came up with the idea of using a round doily to create the pattern for these Lacy Angels.

Roll out a thin slab of white porcelain clay, and then press a doily into it with a rolling pin, picking up all the details of the pattern that you can.

Cut the clay around the doily, which will give you an imprinted circle to work with.

Cut your circle in half, and then cut one of the half circles into two quarter circles [6-1].

Use the half circle to make a standing cone for the body. Place one quarter circle on top of the other, patterned surfaces together. Now cut two wings by making an S-curve with your knife along the curved edge [6-2]. Use the top part of each quarter circle for the sleeves and the bottom parts for the wings.

Now roll a small round ball for the head with an extension for the neck (teardrop shape) [6-3].

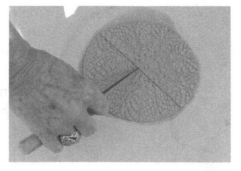

6-1

To assemble the pieces, pinch the head extension into the top of the "body" cone. Roll the two shortest pieces from the quarter circles into "sleeves" and pinch the sleeves into the top of the body, just below the head. Attach the "wings" cut from the quarter circles at the top of the body-cone, in back of the sleeves, taking care not to destroy the doily pattern [6-4].

Now comes the fun of decorating. To create "hair," squeeze a small ball of clay through a garlic press and apply it to the head with a little moisture. (I licked the clay for luck. It's like chalk.) Ripple the skirt a bit and squeeze out two tiny feet, applying them to the edge of the skirt to give the figure a sense of movement. Attach two tiny hands (no detail, just a mitten-like suggestion of hands) to the ends of the sleeves [6-5]. If you want your angel to be a hanging ornament, make a small hole with a knitting needle through the upper part of the wings to give you a place to thread fishing line.

For me, these angels were a wonderful way to preserve my grandmother's doily patterns in clay, as well as a way to offer my customers a

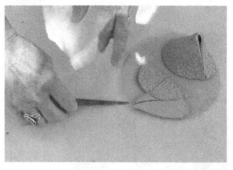

6-2

6-3

6-4

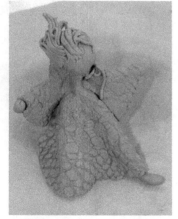

6-5

simple, handmade ornament for Christmas. Once the angels were bone-dry, I quickly dipped them into a transparent white glaze and fired them in and around other pots in my kiln. Over the years, I have probably made more angels than any other single item. My thrifty Dutch grandmother would have been proud!

IMPRINTED BOWLS

Decorating begins with surface textures to enhance the basic shape of any clay form. Start by pinching or throwing five small bowls. While they are still quite wet, deform each one in a different way and add one focal point by pressing something into the surface of the clay (yarn, straw, a button, a hair curler, a comb, an eraser ... even the imprint of a ring).

Variation: Collaborative Reshaping

Do the above exercise with a group of people. Each person shapes and "deforms" one bowl and then passes the deformed bowl on to someone else for texturing. Because this is a group exercise, rather than a product-making experience, these bowls will not be fired. This makes it possible to embed something in the clay (a stone, a ring, a poem). It is important to take some time to talk with your collaborators about this experience.

DECORATIVE RATTLE

Pinch two small bowls and, before you join them, roll some small pellets of clay and put them inside. If your clay is sticky, use a little toilet paper to wrap each pellet so they won't stick together in a lump (the paper will burn away in the firing). Now join the two little bowls by scoring each edge and pressing them firmly together—trapping air inside—to make a small rattle to be used as a rhythm instrument.

Then find an interesting texture outdoors and roll your "rattle" in it to pick up the pattern (things such as boards on a porch, a sidewalk, leaves, rocks, and bark make interesting designs). Quite often these rattles end up looking like weathered stones and may be quite beautiful without further decoration.

Be sure to prick a hole in your "rattle" with a toothpick to let the air escape in drying before you fire your piece. After firing, the "rattle" has a much more percussive sound.

Variation: Unfired Rattle

If you do not plan to fire your rattle, you can fill it with small stones and finish it by burnishing or rubbing it with pastel chalk.

THE LAYERED LOOK

If you are working in a studio or can purchase two different colors of clays (white and red, for instance), there are many ways to create patterns with the clay. You might begin by creating four layers by patting out little slabs of clay—two red and two white—and alternating them like a sandwich [6-6].

6-6

Then press the sandwich together and slice it down the middle, giving you two hunks of red and white clay. Roll each one into a ball and pinch two small bowls—maybe one for a friend who is leaving. The well-known clay artist Paulus Berensohn calls these "beloved bowls."

129

6-7

Pinching will probably wed these two clays together, but you may also find that they separate in drying or firing [6-7]. Clay with a bit of "tooth" or grog will have less tendency to separate. Drying them more slowly than bowls made of a single clay may also help prevent separation.

Variation: Color on Color

Try different ways of layering these clays. Roll a slab of white clay around a fat "snake" of red clay and slice off "cookies" to pinch with. Add one small ball of clay to a center depression, or create strings of dark clay and wrap them around a lighter clay, then divide the ball and pinch two bowls. If you are interested in pursuing this line of inquiry, see Paulus Berensohn's classic book *Finding One's Way with Clay: Pinched Pottery and the Color of Clay.* He has a chart of oxides and suggestions for how they can be added to wet and dry clays for a wide range of colors and inlay designs.

SIMPLE SLIPS

Adding a decorative coating and firing go together. The general term for that coating is a glaze. There are naturally occurring clays that can be used as a glaze because they have the right combination of minerals to stick to most clay bodies through drying, and they will melt at a known temperature.

For many years, it was possible to get clay from Albany, New York, that could be mixed with water and brushed on to make a shiny brown glaze at cone 8 (see chapter 7). Every potter I knew had a good supply of Albany Slip to coat the inside of mugs and bowls for table use. Now the seam has run dry, and it is difficult to find any Albany Slip, so potters are using Cedar Heights Redart Clay instead.

Another matte brown slip that is widely used under other glazes is Barnard Slip. It can be mixed with water and brushed onto bone-dry clay because Barnard will stick to almost anything. Load a Japanese ink brush with Barnard Slip, paint it onto the clay, making sure the color gets into every crevice, and then brush it off the high spots with your hand. This will not only rid your pot of sharp edges (softened by the watery slip), but it will also bring out the texture by reinforcing shadows on the surface. When fired to cone 9 or 10, Barnard has a dark metallic look.

DIG YOUR OWN SLIP

If you live near a known source of clay, you should try local clay as a slip. Near where I grew up in Bellingham, Washington, there were several seams of clay exposed by erosion along Puget Sound. My teacher, Louie Mideke, developed a range of slips made from different clay sources around Whatcom County. Louie Mideke found that he could apply local slips to damp clay and then cut a design through the slip into the body of the pot [6-8].

6-8

Natural slips are usually dark in color, because they contain a variety of heavy minerals; iron and manganese are the most common. These natural combinations can be unique and beautiful and very satisfying to use.

To prepare local clay, follow these steps:
- Dig a small amount (maybe 4 pounds) and spread it out to dry thoroughly.

131

- Pound it to bits with a hammer.
- Grind it to a fine powder with a rolling pin or a mortar and pestle.
- Sieve it through a fine screen to remove rocks and twigs.
- Sieve it onto a small amount of water until all the water is absorbed.
- Test your slip by coating small tiles dried to leather-hardness with one coat, two coats, and three coats. Mark your tiles before you fire them, so you can see how the number of coats affects the outcome.
- Be sure to put your tiles on a small pad of clay or sand in your kiln before firing, in case the slip runs at the temperature of your firing. Keep notes and experiment until you find the right combination of color and texture for your needs.

ENGOBE

An engobe is simply a slip (thick slurry) of the throwing clay with the addition of iron or manganese, maybe 2 percent of each, to create a darker color. Sometimes a frit (a fired and pulverized combination of minerals designed to melt at a specific known temperature) is also added to an engobe to make it melt. By making the colored engobe of the same clay as the pot itself, a good fit is almost guaranteed. An engobe must be applied to leather-hard clay; however, because the pot has already undergone some of its shrinkage, there is some danger that it will peel off. A little corn syrup will help it stick.

If you have access to the supplies of a well-stocked pottery studio, it is possible to make a white engobe out of kaolin and ball clay. In his wonderful reference book *Clay and Glazes for the Potter*, Daniel Rhodes includes a thorough discussion of the variables to help you develop your own slips and engobes.

STAINS

Commercial stains are another way to color raw clay. They can be purchased in small amounts and rubbed or brushed on to bring out a surface texture or create a painted design. Usually stains are covered by a light glaze that will make the clay watertight and smooth to the touch.

BASIC GLAZE

If you are using a slip or an engobe to enhance the texture of your clay, then you might want to experiment with a simple white glaze over the whole piece. To get a glassy coating, you will need to know the firing temperature for the clay and kiln you will be using and work backward to find out which components are needed for the glaze. There are beautiful glazes designed for common firing temperatures also listed in the back of Rhodes's book *Clay and Glazes for the Potter.*

There are also hundreds of well-tested glazes available from local suppliers in 5-pound bags of premixed glaze. If you are not working in a pottery studio with a range of supplies for mixing your own glaze, purchasing one of these glazes would be the way to start. Buy a bag of basic white glaze that fires to the temperature of the kiln to which you have access. Most studios will charge for space in their kilns and may require that you use their glazes so the firing steward will know what is going into the kiln. Check with the kiln source before you purchase your own glaze.

7

Firing

The Crucible of Transformation

Loading the kiln is holy work.
Form and substance change,
creating a new crystalline structure.
Slow cooling completes the process.

Firing is an act of commitment that touches something primal in me. I am attracted by the fire's warmth and dancing light, but instinct tells me to pull away when fire gets too close because I know it burns, consumes, and kills. That is, indeed, what happens to the clay: organic matter burns away and only stone is left, a new crystalline structure that is sometimes so dense and thin that it rings like a chime.

Closing the kiln leaves no room for indecision. I must commit the pots I love to the fire's consuming power without recourse to rescue if something unexpected happens. Waiting for the heat to do its work is a discipline born of experience. There are no shortcuts. I must see the process through to the end. Remembering past results helps me take the time necessary for the fire to complete the process I have started. The prize for this commitment is transformation—a new internal structure—but to get that, I must let go of my control and trust change to a power greater than my own.

When I have only a few pots and want to get them through the process, I feel poor, and I am anxious that the firing turn out well. But when I have enough pots to choose the optimum combination for each shelf, I feel rich and full, ready to commit what I have brought this far to the transforming heat of the kiln.

SORTING

When I am ready to let go of what my hands have made and trust the fire to do its work, I begin to sort the pots by size. I check each pot to make sure there is no glaze on the bottom rim, which would fuse it to the shelf during the firing. I examine the glaze coat to make sure there are no bare spots where the glaze dried away from the clay and dropped off, no chips or cracks that would guarantee failure. Sometimes I can repair small flaws if I take the time to do it.

The empty chamber waits, pristine with a coat of kiln wash to keep runny glazes from bonding to the shelf. If glaze does run, the pot must be chipped off of the kiln shelf—with the risk of breaking it. And once the pot is separated, the kiln wash will have to be ground off of the finished pot with a diamond drill. It's better to take precautions at the beginning to prevent those things from happening, if possible. Here, carefulness is not a sign of timidity. It's practical to check those details.

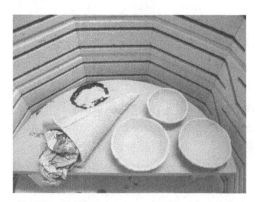

Stacking a kiln.

Sorting and stacking the kiln is a ritual of preparation, methodical and precise. It's like sorting laundry, unloading groceries, practicing the piano before a recital, or doing the research before a court case. I place each pot close to others of similar height for best heat conduction.

After I load one shelf, I place three stilts on it to hold the next higher shelf, and I repeat the process, loading another shelf until the kiln is full. Many kilns have room to stack four or five shelves this way, one on top of the other.

Because all heat rises, stacking the kiln is done to maximize heat flow in and around the pots and still be efficient about the use of fuel. Decisions about where to place a pot represent some combination of the shape and glaze and efficiency of loading. Since most studio kilns are top-loading kilns, reaching the bottom level can be a chore, so most potters put their larger pieces on the bottom (although that is likely to be a little cooler than the middle or top of the kiln because heat rises and collects under the lid).

If the shelves are warped from many firings, or if the stilts have picked up a bit of grit or kiln wash so that they do not stand absolutely straight, the stack of shelves can be precarious. Yet there is something comforting about the closeness of these pots, as if they stand together before some fearsome threat, for radical change always flirts with extinction. Preparing the kiln reminds me how often routines and risk go hand in hand. In fact, the very reason we need to practice certain skills (such as driving a car or riding a bicycle) is that mistakes can be disastrous.

Maybe that is why the process of sorting has something of a mythic quality, where the innocents face great danger. Fairy tales are full of heroines who must separate straw from wheat or find a needle in a haystack, or heroes who must decipher a hidden message or steal a key. In mythic sorting, the hero or heroine finally has to face "the fire" alone, without the aid of mechanical assists, and rely on individual resourcefulness and creativity. Luke Skywalker, in the twentieth-century mythological story of *Star Wars*, for example, had to turn off the automatic pilot as he came to the end of a perilous chase, in order to navigate with his intuition.

Clarissa Pinkola Estés includes many sorting tasks in her compendium of archetypal stories *Women Who Run with the Wolves: Myths and Stories of the Wild Woman Archetype*. She describes sorting as "making fine distinctions" and "observing the power of the unconscious and how it works even when the ego is not aware." What we learn from those stories is that the world is full of false choices, that we are not born wise, and that discernment can be developed.

The sorting that Dr. Estés describes in the tale of Vasalisa is something that most of us have done: we face a question or a dilemma that seems to have no answer, we leave it alone (or fall asleep), and then, when we come back to it, we find a good answer waiting. It's a way of cultivating the unconscious, relying on our intuition, or remembering a long-forgotten fact. We can learn to trust this way of sorting, even if we do not understand it ... if we are also willing to find no good answer waiting.

The soulwork of sorting involves learning to trust other kinds of knowing beyond reason and logic. It is an aspect of decision making that relies on unseen and sometimes unknown powers. But sorting doesn't mean that we leave our brains behind. Thinking and feeling are both needed for the wisdom of sorting.

When I am sorting pots for the kiln, if my intuition tells me that a pot is not really made well, or that the lid does not really fit, this is the time to set it aside. Firing is not just about the individual pots but also about the whole kiln load. If one pot blows apart or the glaze runs onto the shelf, it can affect the other pots in the kiln. Sorting gives me another chance to let go of what I do not need, what will only become a burden later.

As I am loading the kiln, I am also thinking about the effects that different glazes have on each other. Some glazes are "fugitive," because they tend to hop from one pot to another. In other cases, one glaze melts more readily than another, so I can plan where to put it in the kiln for best results. I am also thinking about what I require for a show or sale, or simply for a special person in need.

Loading a kiln can be a reminder that thoughtful preparation is the handmaiden of mystery. Even mundane tasks, approached as a spiritual practice, can help us learn to trust the soul's knowing. At its heart, sorting is about knowing when to act—and how.

Knowing When to Act—and How

- How do you practice sorting in everyday life?

- Where do you tend to get stuck? Are there places in your house (or your life) where you are avoiding the task of sorting?

- What does that tell you about your inner work of completion and closure?

WAITING

When the shelves of the kiln are loaded to my satisfaction, I place three cones in a pad of clay and set them where I can see them through a peephole in the wall of the kiln. The cones, made of clay that is specially mixed to melt at specific temperatures, are a better measure of heat applied over time than a mechanical thermometer is. I check to make sure the cones are visible, and then I brick up the door, sealing the pots inside so the firing chamber acts like part of the chimney.

It is time to apply the heat. Electricity is the most common source, but actual fire (using gas, wood, dung, or manure) provides a more active environment—with more unknowns. Firing a gas kiln begins slowly so the surface water on the clay can evaporate rather than boil the clay apart. Waiting for the kiln to heat slowly takes discipline and experience. The process is tedious and exacting. I am always tempted to hurry, to finish early so I can be done with the tension. Once again, the temptation to hurry must be tempered. There is nothing comfortable about the process of transformation, and it is a reminder that basic change takes time—and often heat. There is no microwave shortcut. It is only high heat over time that will turn clay into a ceramic substance.

At first, a gas firing is pure sound. The burners roar like a propane torch. The kiln is pitch-black inside. I must hold the temperature just below the boiling point because at 212°F, the point at which water turns to steam, glaze can pop off and damp pots can explode. I check for surface steam, using a mirror held to the peephole, and when no more water condenses on the mirror, I begin to push the temperature upward more rapidly.

As the temperature climbs, an orange glow begins to appear as the pots heat up. As more heat is applied, the color inside the kiln changes to bright yellow and, finally, to a white heat. By this time, day has turned to night, and the whole kiln glows and roars in the darkness.

When the temperature climbs over 2,000°F, I reduce the oxygen by closing the burner ports while still allowing enough air in to keep the fire burning hot. Reducing the oxygen creates a smoky atmosphere that affects both color and crystal development of the soft and viscous glazes. Tongues of flame reach for air out of every crack in the kiln, and it looks like a devouring dragon reaching for air to keep its fury going. In this final stage, the kiln has its own fiery spirit and its own timing for the work of transformation taking place inside.

Like a sentry posted to guard and yet still encourage the dragon's breath, I watch through the peephole until all three cones bend, telling me that the chemical change in clay and glaze has been completed. Then I turn off the burners, block the ports so that cool air cannot crack the pots, and seal the other openings. My long vigil is over. I am often exhausted and glad to sleep when a firing is finished.

But the waiting is not over yet. Just as I waited for the pots to heat, now I must wait again to see what the fire has done. This waiting stands like a silent word from nature against our cultural pressure for instant results. Slow cooling is as important as slow heating for these rock crystals to form without cracking. From a translucent and nearly liquid state, the clay and glaze must restabilize. I learn again that transformation takes time.

Relationships are like this too. Sometimes I shortchange the process, leaving an uncomfortable situation before the inner work is done. But other times, I have been able to stay with a situation or relationship as it changes from the inside out. I believe that's what happened with my mother.

About the time I went off to college, my mother began drinking secretly. She was in her early forties, restless and angry about the "waste" of her Stanford education. Whenever things got tense at home, she dozed on the couch in an alcoholic stupor. Visiting my parents became more problematic, although my mother did not drink constantly, and there were good times when she was sober. Even though I was long past needing her physical care, I felt angry and betrayed because she was not the mother I had grown up with.

Then, when I was nearly forty, Faith at Work offered me a model of confession based on the 12-step recovery movement. I began to explore my feelings of anger and abandonment within the small circles of trust that Faith at Work offered. The structure of temporary community helped me reclaim a fuller range of my feelings in a safe space. Waiting for my mother to change seemed futile, so I concentrated on making better decisions in the only life I could control: my own. As I did my own inner work, I began to feel a subtle shift in my feelings toward my mother. Even though she was still drinking, I began to feel my love for her alongside my anger at the wasted opportunities for relationship.

Then, after my father died, my mother went into a nine-week treatment program. At seventy-four, she not only got sober but also began to recover her soul. Although I am no expert, I do think there is something about bottled spirits (alcohol) being a substitute for internal spiritual hunger. But for me, the important piece was the internal work I had been doing. In the "slow cooling time" of her recovery, I discovered that I could respond with gladness to her sobriety. We had nearly twenty years to build a relationship after she got sober, and I can say truthfully that I began "falling in love with my mother." It was a process that took time and steady attention without any guarantee of success. Like firing a kiln load of pots, the transformation was internal. The dream I had earlier, of holding her on my lap, rocking in the moon's circle with the quilt tucked around us, felt like the completion of that inner journey.

All living things require waiting for the cycles of growth and harvest, healing and dying. Although we can encourage these cycles, we do not control them. Machines have allowed us to be more efficient, making us more impatient about waiting for anything. It's not "efficient," for example, to bake cookies, to let sourdough bread rise, to smoke a turkey, or to knit a scarf. They all take time—and love. We could purchase these things already made, but the energy and attention that it takes to make these things by hand would be lost, and our glimpse of ordinary transformation would be shortchanged.

Soulwork is a slow transformation process involving the trust, patience, and hope of waiting. As Parker Palmer writes in *Let Your Life Speak: Listening for the Voice of Vocation*, the soul is "like a wild animal—tough, resilient, savvy, self-sufficient, and yet exceedingly shy." And if we know anything about wanting to attract a wild animal, then waiting quietly would be at the top of the list.

Patience is not highly valued in our culture, yet we all experience many ordinary things that take time and require a great deal of patience. When waiting is simply something we must do, such as at a doctor's office or while the clothes are drying, what might it be like to see that time as a gift rather than a waste? A time when we could do something that we love to do? Knitting, quilting, and reading come to mind. Even waiting for a stoplight to turn green could be an occasion for breathing consciously, for renewal and awareness amid the day's pressing activities. When I'm waiting in line for airport security, I have a choice: I can be angry and impatient, or I can remember to breathe and smile. The image I have in those moments is that my body can be a chamber of soulwork, of transforming fire.

Most of the time when we are waiting, we are waiting for something to happen, for "results." Too much emphasis on expected results can bring disappointment, even despair, yet without a visible purpose, waiting can become simply a state of passivity. This is where I draw hope from waiting for the kiln. As I wait for the firing, and wait for the cooling, I experience waiting not as a passive stance, but as an active pause—even a participant—in the dance of creativity. The soulwork of clay allows me to see waiting as part of a longer process that gives it meaning and perspective. Practicing patience again and again at the door of the kiln is a reminder to stand at the door of life's surprises as well.

Waiting with Purpose

- Think of some of the ordinary activities that you do that involve waiting: waiting for the children to come home from school, waiting for the clothes to dry, or waiting in the checkout line at the grocery store or post office. Is there something you could do to see your waiting time as a gift?

- What are you waiting for in your life? Perhaps for children to grow up, a project to be completed, work to begin (or end), a move you need or want to make. Is there something you could do to remind yourself of the larger purpose of your waiting?

TRANSFORMATION

Finally, it is time to open the kiln, to release the pots from their crucible of transformation. As I open the lid, light enters and sparkles on gleaming surfaces where before there had been only the chalky dust of powdered minerals. Fire has transformed each pot into its unique beauty.

The pots are still warm as I cup each one in my hands, examining it like a newborn. As I stand in the cool morning air, warmed by the firebricks still giving off heat, I remember my hopes for each special glaze, and I look for results. Sometimes I am surprised by an unexpected blush of color or a blemish that I didn't plan for. No matter how often I fire, opening the kiln is always an experience full of wonder. Nothing is just what I planned for it to be.

When I was learning to pot, Louie fired his ancient gas kiln every other week. It took him twenty-four hours to fire the kiln and two days for it to cool down enough so we could handle the pots. Early on Saturday morning, while it was still dark, I would drive out to Louie and Jean's place as the sun began to tint the horizon. It was usually cold enough to see my breath, so the warmth of the kiln shed was a good place to be. Together, Louie and I would unbrick the door, stacking the arch bricks carefully so they wouldn't crumble at the edges. Our ritual was to complete the task of unbricking the whole door before we would take any pot out—another experience of waiting.

As the line of bricks got lower, we could begin to see the glistening pots inside, and our excitement rose. It was always a chamber full of surprises. The colors were breathtaking: turquoise, blood red, rich iron reds, and lustrous ocean greens. Louie would hand me the pots, one at a time, to cradle in my hands, and we would exclaim over each one's beauty and look at its flaws. When all the shelves had been emptied, we would usually take five or six of the best pots into the house and put them on the kitchen table to enjoy while we ate breakfast together. It was a sacred time, a ritual I never got tired of. And I know it was richer for being shared.

Celebrations

- How do you celebrate "small" passages in your life or mark special events? Are there special smells or tastes that you associate with celebration? What makes you feel happy, celebrative, joyful?

- Think about how you celebrate major transitions in your life. What do you usually do to celebrate them? Who is usually present? Are there other people you would like to include in future celebrations? Other ways you would like to celebrate?

- If you are coming to a time of completion (a child moving out of the house, finishing a project, changing jobs or leaving a job, moving, downsizing), what celebratory rituals might be helpful? Who would you want to be there?

RELEASE

In the beginning, I had the impulse to keep my cherished creations close by. But if I kept all the pots I've made over the years, I would be drowning in them! So I have practiced a different kind of love, that of letting go as a spiritual discipline. With my pottery, it was as simple as putting a price tag on each pot as soon as I had the kiln unloaded. I inspected the pots and priced them to sell at the cooperative studio that I shared at the Torpedo Factory. Making that a routine helped me from getting too attached to any particular piece. I have saved very few pots from that period of my work.

Release is a peculiar discipline because, without the earlier stages of creative participation, releasing can simply be a symptom of our throwaway culture. If nothing is valued, release is no virtue. But if we have engaged fully in the soulwork of grounding and centering, shaping and finishing, then release is another challenge. Letting go of things (plans, objects, people, pots) is part of a larger rhythm of creativity in the universe. Acknowledging the importance of releasing is part of the process that we need in order to make room for new life.

Now that I am making unfired burial urns, they call for a ritual of release that is not as commercial as selling my pots. I no longer imagine that people will be using these vessels over time. The whole purpose of making unfired burial urns is to let them return to the earth "from whence they came." My emphasis has shifted from the pot itself to the importance of a final sacred ritual for the ashes of a loved one. It brings me back to the idea of art and usefulness going hand in hand from the beginning of human consciousness.

For every one of us on the human journey, death is the final release. But it is much more complex than just the physical release of the life spirit from the body. Endings are part of a greater story that transcends our individual lives. We do not know the journey on which this particular crucible of transformation will take us, but we do know that we want to be "let go" with care and attention. I hear more people these days talking about wanting to be "scattered" in a place that they have loved. As people more consciously take these sacred ending rituals into their own hands, wanting green burials, my urns are finding a place in this growing movement.

For those of us whose lives continue on after the death of a loved one, release takes on even deeper dimensions. Release is not only a way of honoring the life process, expressing love, and saying good-bye; it is also a way of celebrating all the life stages that went into revealing the unique beauty of our loved one's soul. Rituals of remembrance can help us release the person's physical presence without taking away his or her spiritual essence.

I think of the people who came to my mother's memorial service at the retirement center. Some were staff members who helped care for her. Others came not because they knew my mother well, but because they needed a ritual of release for other deaths they were carrying. We had structured the service to include stories from the participants about my mother, and when the service was over, one of her regular eating companions asked if he could show me some pictures of his wife and three children, whom he had outlived. I was touched by his desire to add his own story to the ritual we had created for my mother, and as we talked, I learned that he had been unable to attend his wife's funeral.

Surely listening to each other's stories, as well as telling our own, is a gift of release that we can give freely, even easily. Yet individualism is such a high-priority value in our culture that we may be reluctant to "invade someone else's space," or we may feel we need to "respect their privacy."

Although the phrase "You can do it!" might well be the affirmation slogan of our time, the underbelly of this position is "What happens when I *can't?*" Or, what happens when the one we're counting on *can't?* If we have placed individualism at the pinnacle of self-sufficiency, then we may be just a little out of practice when it comes to giving and receiving help. I think the release of individualism may well be one of the most growth-filled steps we can take on the soulwork journey, and sharing our stories may be a good place to start.

Tell Me a Story

- Most of us can remember a favorite story from childhood, but do you have a favorite book or movie, maybe a poem, that helps you release tensions or disappointments now? Is there someone with whom you might share this?

- Is there a room in your house or a corner in your apartment where things tend to accumulate? Do you know someone who could help you clear out that space and share whatever stories might be stored there?

- Transformation is not always easy or even welcome. Can you recall a change that came unexpectedly but had major consequences for you? Who did you tell about it? What is the story you tell about that event now? Do you have an "artifact" from that transition? Where is the artifact now? What does its placement tell you?

BACK TO THE BEGINNING

Firing takes us back to the beginning, to the composition of clay itself. It was human ingenuity that figured out how to harden clay with fire, even if it happened by accident to begin with. Because clay and fuel occur naturally all over the world, pottery developed wherever humans clustered together. Clay tablets became the first writing paper. Clay vessels stored grain, and clay roof tiles made houses more water-resistant. Fired clay recorded our first words and our first artistry.

To fire clay, traditional potters used open fires fueled by grass, dung, wood, or a combination of those fuels. Because there was no good way to slow down the supply of oxygen with these open fires, the clay vessels had to withstand a great deal of thermal shock when fired. Therefore, the type of fuel available often determined how the clay could be used.

Traditional potters would usually mix several local clays to make it ready for the fuel to which they had access. The location of "good clay" and the proper ratio for mixing it with other materials became traditions that were handed down within families and clans. In Japan and China, some of those traditional recipes go back many generations. Clay became a significant part of those cultures because their geography and climate provided a combination of fine secondary clay (washed far from its primary source) and dense wood (such as teak) that would fire to a very high temperature. They developed kilns to contain the heat and control the atmosphere inside. Other peoples, such as the Babylonians and Egyptians, developed kilns as early as 5000 BCE. In other parts of the world, the natural clay was full of mica or sand, and could withstand a quick, hot fire of grass, so these cultures developed different methods of firing by stacking pots on the open ground and surrounding them with fuel.

There are also many natural clays that can be worked without cracking but do not hold together in a fast fire. With these clays, a potter can either slow down the fire to let a fine-grained clay mature without exploding, or add a tempering agent (such as sand, grog, or volcanic ash) to space out the clay molecules. This would make the clay less pliable for throwing on a wheel but useful for coiling and pinching, the traditional method for making pots without a wheel.

The demands of firing influence shape and decoration as well. From the beginning, burnishing, rather than glazing, helped harden the body without adding another material that might expand and shrink at a different rate than the clay. Round shapes, too, withstood thermal shock more easily than square shapes with joints to crack open.

Today, museums are full of clay pots and figurines that show an amazing range of human ingenuity and resourcefulness when it comes to shaping and firing clay. We know, too, that many more ceramics lie broken in layers of past civilizations, waiting to be found. I hope you will spend some time in your local museum, looking at these earliest artifacts with the eyes of your soul. Let your heart open to the long line of artisans who carried the traditions of working with clay from then into now.

If you have tried some of the clay projects in this book, you will no doubt have learned some of the same things that potters have learned for generations. Perhaps you have a new way to appreciate what these traditional potters were able to accomplish and pass down through the generations.

I am also hoping that the questions and clay projects in each chapter have awakened your longing for direct experience with handwork that can invite your soul out to play again. We were all mud-loving children once, but when we learned to read and think, most of us put away those activities as being childish. Yet there is a good reason why nearly every culture has a creation story that begins with clay: it calls us forth as nothing else does. By using clay, every one of us can experience, in a relatively short time, the thrill of creating something from a shapeless, formless mass.

We are indeed creatures of the earth and creators of possibilities. Working with clay is a way to get our hands dirty and our minds clear. To reclaim an elemental sense of connection with the earth itself. To bring us home to our bodies. To express our soul's longing for life. To reclaim the sacred act of creation as essential to our wholeness. This is the soulwork of clay.

Try It with Clay!

Heat applied to clay over time will harden any clay body, but thermal shock always makes firing risky, if not dangerous. The first rule for firing, then, is to *know your clay*. Start small. Test often and keep notes on your method of firing. Anyone who has used an unglazed clay pot for cooking knows that you must begin with your dish in a cold oven to let it heat up evenly. The same principle must be observed when firing clay. Don't put an unfired pot in a red-hot fire, because it will probably explode from moisture trapped in the clay.

There are many fine books available about the composition of clay and techniques for different kinds of firing, so I have limited the exercises here to projects that you can do with a minimum of fuss and equipment.

DAMP CLAY FIRING

Some clay is quite tolerant of open flames when it is still damp. You won't know that unless you are willing to risk cracking a damp clay pot to experiment. In a retreat setting, I once brought smooth-grained white clay, designed to fire at cone 6 (a common way of designating the ideal firing temperature). The body was very plastic and easy to use, so we used it for a number of exercises. As the weekend came to a close, I wanted to use one of the pots I had made during the weekend as a receptacle for burning our prayers. I asked people to write a prayer on a slip of paper, and we lit them one at a time and placed them in the damp clay pot [7-1].

7-1

The clay warmed but did not break, and when we were finished, the inside of the pot had a lovely gray-brown finish. Since then, I have learned that this particular clay has a very wide tolerance for heat shock, and I've used it for most of the following projects.

If you have purchased a bag of clay, you can experiment with its heat tolerance by pinching a small bowl. Let it dry until it is leather-hard. Write your own prayer of release on a small strip of paper, light it, and place it in the bowl to test its resilience—and yours. The bowl may well crack or explode from the shock of open flames, so do not hold the bowl in your hand unless you are very familiar with the clay.

FIREPLACE FIRING

Do you have a brick fireplace in your house? If so, you are seeing fired clay in its most common form—as insulating brick. Bricks were once handmade wherever clay occurred naturally and fired in an open fire or a simple kiln (oven) made of other bricks to contain the heat longer.

It's a good idea to test firing your clay in an open fireplace with something small—maybe a small pinched bowl or beads made of different clays. Make sure that it is bone-dry by putting it against your cheek. If it's cool, there is still moisture in the clay. You can dry off any surface moisture by putting your piece in the oven at 200°F (below boiling) for 30 minutes or so. The warmth will help your clay withstand any heat shock from the open flames in your fireplace.

Once you are sure that your piece is dry, put it in a protected place in the fireplace before you start the fire. Placing the warmed pot against the back wall or under the andiron is a good idea because a wood fire will drop pieces of charcoal as well as ash. Start your fire and leave your piece in its spot until the fire has burned out.

A piece fired this way will probably be grayish or black, depending on the clay and the amount of oxygen available to the fire. After the piece is cool, you can brush off the ashes carefully and then rub the piece with paste wax and buff it for a little shine. Clay fired this way will not be very durable, because the heat does not last long enough at a high temperature to melt whatever glass component is in the clay, but it can be fun and easy to try.

Variation: Using a Foil Envelope

Try wrapping your clay piece in aluminum foil to create a smoky fire inside. If the pot has been burnished, be careful about scratching the surface if you cover it this way.

CHARCOAL GRILL FIRING

You can also use your backyard charcoal grill to experiment with firing. It arouses less suspicion among suburban neighbors than a smoldering garbage can full of sawdust (see below)!

A round canister-type grill provides the most even firing. Preheating your clay piece in the oven will help it withstand the heat shock of a fire made with charcoal briquettes.

Use one of those metal chimneys available at the hardware store to start your briquettes. Put crumbled paper at the bottom of your grill, under the grate. Then pile some unlit briquettes on the grate and up around the edges, forming a kind of nest for your pots [7-2]. Put your preheated pots directly on the unlit briquettes and pour the glowing briquettes from your fire-starter chimney on top of the unlit briquettes, next to the wall of the grill. Then use a match

7-2

153

7-3

to light the crumbled paper at the bottom so your unlit briquettes will be ignited by heat from both sides [7-3].

Use the lid and bottom vents to control the amount of oxygen and therefore the amount of flame. Once the charcoal is burning well and all the coals are red-hot, close the lid (and maybe the vents, too) to smoke the pots at the end of the firing. When cool to the touch, brush the ash away with a soft cloth and finish with a coat of paste wax [7-4].

Variation: Sawdust Logs

You can increase the heat of a charcoal fire by slicing one or two sawdust logs and putting them around your pots.

Variation: Common Glaze Materials

7-4

Experiment with glaze materials from your kitchen by sprinkling each pot with something different—sea salt, epsom salt, borax—or wrapping a piece in colored newspaper (the comic section). You may be surprised at the results. Make notes about what you use where, so if you like what happens, you can use the same technique again. (Another word of caution: avoid breathing these vapors; the smoke is not good for you.)

Variation: Garden Manure

You can fill your pots with dried manure, commonly available from a garden supply store as fertilizer. Or experiment with adding manure on top of the briquettes once they are burning well. The manure will tend to smother the fire, but it adds some other interesting components.

154

SAWDUST FIRING

Another way of firing pots in your backyard is to use sawdust as the fuel. This is my favorite way of firing burnished pots because the fire smolders naturally, unless the sawdust is very coarse—then it will burn quickly with a clear, bright flame. It is usually possible to find sawdust at a lumberyard or from a hardwood artisan, free for the taking (I usually bring a batch of cookies for this happy exchange). Do *not* get your sawdust from a store where the sawdust might contain resins and epoxies from sawing plywood.

You'll need to make walls for your sawdust kiln out of cement blocks or regular bricks, stacking the walls high enough to accommodate whatever clay pieces you have made. The advantage of this method is that you can easily change the size and shape of your kiln.

Pour 3 or 4 inches of sawdust in the bottom (on the ground), and then begin loading your pots. Remember that the sawdust will burn during the firing, so you must expect the higher pots to settle down onto the lower ones. I usually load my biggest pieces on the bottom, filling them first with sawdust and then inverting them, rim down. I also put smaller pots or figures inside of larger pots for protection.

You can also experiment with color by crumpling the comic section of the newspaper around or in a pot to see whether you get some color flashing that way. Salt will also work, and seaweed or leaves may produce interesting colors.

Put 2 to 3 inches of sawdust between pots and between layers of pots. If you are firing a single large pot, place it in the middle of the kiln with plenty of sawdust on all sides. Then crumple newspapers all over the top of the sawdust and light the fire in several places. Once it is burning well and the sawdust has started to burn, put a lid on it (you can use a kiln shelf or a large baking sheet) and let it smolder until the fire goes out.

The pot in figure 7-5 was fired with sawdust in an open pit with a very fast, hot flame. The clay contained lots of mica, which

7-5

7-6

is very tolerant of heat shock, so when we removed the pots from the fire, they were still quite hot. We draped horsehair on the surface (long human hair would also work), and it sizzled into the funny shape you see here as a black line.

Variation: Garbage Can Kiln

Instead of using cement blocks for the walls of your sawdust kiln, you can purchase a galvanized garbage can and make a light, transportable kiln [7-6]. You *must* drill or punch holes in the garbage can to provide enough air for sawdust to burn. It is especially important to have vent holes in the bottom and around the bottom of the kiln. I usually put three or four rings of 1-inch holes around the can with a metal drill. (Leaving the lid on while you do the drilling will help stabilize the can. You do not need holes in the lid because you can leave it ajar to increase the oxygen at the beginning of the firing.)

The advantage of having a ring of holes around the can is that you can see at a glance how far the fire has burned down in the can. If a wind comes up and the fire is going too fast, just wrap the garbage can kiln with aluminum foil to slow down the air intake.

ELECTRIC KILN

Most studio potters have access to an electric kiln. It's a significant purchase, and if you want to use it inside, it must be vented. It also requires special heavy-duty wiring for the current needed, similar to your stove or dryer hookup.

To stabilize a piece of dried clay, most people "biscuit fire" (or bisque) their ware before glazing. That means bringing the clay up to 932°F–1,112°F—something that can be done with precision in an electric kiln that has a built-in temperature gauge. The critical stages in a bisque firing are these:

- Up to 212°F, the surface water of plasticity is driven off as vapor. The greatest risk of explosion occurs in thick pieces during this portion of the firing.
- Between 212°F and 392°F, organic materials begin to burn out.
- At 1,063°F, there is a quartz inversion in the clay itself, and chemically combined water is lost. A new ceramic material is thus formed at this temperature.
- A bisque firing to 1,742°F will leave stoneware or porcelain clay porous enough to absorb glaze applied by dipping or spraying it on. The final firing will usually be around 2,372°F for those clays.

Because many open fires or sawdust firings do not reach even 932°F, the first quartz inversion does not take place, and the pots are not technically a stable ceramic material. But at temperatures much above 1,270°F, burnished clay will lose its shiny surface. One way to get stability *and* a burnished surface is to bisque fire to a higher temperature and then cover the piece with slip, which is then burnished and refired at a lower temperature.

Most people who use an electric kiln for both bisque firing and glaze firing are not looking for the slow rhythms of burnished pots or the unknowns of an open fire. An electric kiln is the most predictable method of firing and the most neutral as well. Almost all commercially made ceramic ware is fired in an electric kiln.

GAS KILN

Many potters like to fire with natural or bottled gas (LPG) because of the chemically active atmosphere that it produces at very high temperatures. As with wood, the fire can burn hot and clean when there is plenty of oxygen (sometimes added with the blower), and a smoky atmosphere can be created for reduction firing (reducing the amount of oxygen available to the fire). Under those conditions, iron in the clay will spot through the glaze, giving it a mottled appearance, and copper can produce a stunning magenta glaze. Many studio potters prefer the unknowns of reduction firing simply because it is less predictable and the surface of glazes look more like natural stone than a commercial glaze.

I had a small gas kiln that was about the size of a 55-gallon drum because local zoning regulations said that if I built a kiln from scratch, it would be considered an "exterior structure," but if I purchased a ready-made kiln, it was treated as a gas appliance (i.e., a gas grill). I took the easy way out and bought a gas kiln. There was nothing else in my life that felt as holy and mysterious as firing my gas kiln at night. During a firing, I would get up every couple of hours to turn it up, or watch for the cones bending to signify the end of a firing. Then I could turn off the burners, seal up the openings, and drop into bed with a sense of having witnessed transformation once again.

I probably fired that little gas kiln a thousand times before the bricks got so brittle and soft that they began to disintegrate. When that happened, I crumbled the bricks with my hands and spaded them into the garden. In all that time, I never did a bisque firing. Instead, I worked with slips and glazes until they fit my raw clay pots without flaking off, and then fired them just once, to cone 9 or 10, for a single chemical bond between clay and glaze. Now, with rising fuel prices, potters are working hard to lower firing temperatures and be more conscious of pollution without losing the strong tradition of studio pottery that has grown up in the United States.

Whichever type of firing you use, whichever shapes and glazes and techniques you experiment with, let your mind and heart and body always come back to the hands-on spirituality of clay. I think again of one of my favorite M. C. Richards quotations: "It is not the pots we are forming, but ourselves." Trust the process, lean into the possibilities, and follow the journey of discovery that is the soulwork of clay.

Epilogue

Now that I've finished writing the clay exercises for the "Try It with Clay" section of each chapter, I find myself hoping that you have indeed gotten clay into your own hands at some point. It's one thing to read about the amazing properties of clay—pliability in the wet form and then stability in the dry form—but it's quite another thing to try it for yourself.

Even though this hands-on approach to spirituality might not become a regular practice for you of working with clay, the questions which emerge from each of the seven chapters might be something to work with over time. The questions will remind you of the journey we have traveled together in this book, and be another way to add your story to the ongoing stream of creation and creativity.

Give yourself the joyful task of answering these questions with clay or color, with words or pictures, with stories or poetry, or any other form of expression that you can think of.

1. Where and how do you feel grounded on this planet?
2. How are you being kneaded by pressures outside of yourself?
3. What actions or practices are centering for you?
4. Who or what are the inner and outer pressures that shape your life?

5. How do you know when some piece of your life is finished? How do you mark that?

6. When do you play? Celebrate? Enjoy community? With whom do you share your imagination?

7. If firing tends to fix certain forms over time, which fires (transforming experiences) have made you who you are?

Blessings on your path,
Marjory Zoet Bankson

Suggestions for Further Reading

BASIC BOOKS FOR WORKING WITH CLAY

Bager, Bertel. *Nature as Designer: A Botanical Art Study*. New York: Van Nostrand Reinhold, 1966.

Ball, F. Carlton, and Janice Lovoos. *Making Pottery without a Wheel: Texture and Form in Clay*. New York: Van Nostrand Reinhold, 1974.

Berensohn, Paulus. *Finding One's Way with Clay: Pinched Pottery and the Color of Clay*. New York: Simon & Schuster, 1972.

Counts, Charles. *Pottery Workshop: A Study in the Making of Pottery*. New York: MacMillan, 1976.

Fournier, Robert. *Illustrated Dictionary of Practical Pottery*. New York: KP Books, 2000.

Giorgini, Frank. *Handmade Tiles: Designing, Making, Decorating*. New York: Sterling, 2001.

Harvey, Roger, and John and Sylvia Kolb. *Building Pottery Equipment*. New York: Watson-Guptill, 1975.

Leach, Bernard. *Potter's Book*. London: Faber and Faber, 1988.

Nelson, Glenn C., and Richard Burkett. *Ceramics: A Potter's Handbook*. Clifton Park, NY: Wadsworth, 2001.

Obstler, Mimi. *Out of the Earth into the Fire: A Course in Ceramic Materials for the Studio Potter*, 2nd Edition. Westerville, OH: The American Ceramic Society, 2001.

Perryman, Jane. *Smoke Firing: Contemporary Artists and Approaches.* Philadelphia: University of Pennsylvania Press, 2008.

Peterson, Susan. *The Living Tradition of Maria Martinez.* Bunkyo-ku, Tokyo: Kodansha International, 1992.

Rhodes, Daniel. Revised and expanded by Robin Hopper. *Clay and Glazes for the Potter*, 3rd Edition. Iola, WI: KP Books, 2000.

———. *Kilns, Design, Construction, and Operation.* Clifton Park, NY: Chilton Book, 1986.

———. *Pottery Form.* Mineola, NY: Dover, 2004.

———. *Stoneware and Porcelain: The Art of High-Fired Pottery.* Clifton Park, NY: Chilton Book, 1959.

Riegger, Hal. *Primitive Pottery.* New York: Van Nostrand Reinhold, 1972.

Von Dassow, Sumi, ed. *Barrel, Pit, and Saggar Firing: A Collection of Articles from Ceramics Monthly.* Westerville, OH: The American Ceramics Society, 2001.

BOOKS THAT INSPIRED THE SOULWORK OF CLAY

Allen, Pat B. *Art Is a Way of Knowing.* Boston: Shambhala, 1995.

Eliot, T. S. *The Complete Poems and Plays, 1909–1950.* San Diego: Harcourt, 1952.

Estés, Clarissa Pinkola. *Women Who Run with the Wolves: Myths and Stories of the Wild Woman Archetype.* New York: Random House, 1996.

Hillman, James. *The Dream and the Underworld.* New York: HarperCollins, 1979.

———. *The Soul's Code: In Search of Character and Calling.* New York: Grand Central, 1997.

Oliver, Mary. *New and Selected Poems: Volume One.* Boston: Beacon Press, 2005.

Palmer, Parker J. *Let Your Life Speak: Listening for the Voice of Vocation.* San Francisco: Jossey-Bass, 1999.

Richards, Mary C. *Centering: In Pottery, Poetry and the Person*. Middletown, CT: Wesleyan University Press, 1989.

———. *Imagine Inventing Yellow: New and Selected Poems*. Barrytown, NY: Barrytown/Station Hill, 1991.

———. *Opening Our Moral Eye: Essays, Talks, and Poems Embracing Creativity and Community*. Great Barrington, MA: Steiner Books, 1996.

Project Index

Important Terms and Processes Index

Notes

Children's Spirituality—Board Books

Adam and Eve's New Day (A Board Book)
by Sandy Eisenberg Sasso; Full-color illus. by Joani Keller Rothenberg
A lesson in hope for every child who has worried about what comes next. Abridged from *Adam and Eve's First Sunset*.
5 x 5, 24 pp, Full-color illus., Board Book, 978-1-59473-205-8 **$7.99** *For ages 0–4*

How Did the Animals Help God? (A Board Book)
by Nancy Sohn Swartz; Full-color illus. by Melanie Hall
Abridged from *In Our Image*, God asks all of nature to offer gifts to humankind—with a promise that they will care for creation in return.
5 x 5, 24 pp, Board Book, Full-color illus., 978-1-59473-044-3 **$7.99** *For ages 0–4*

Where Is God? (A Board Book) *by Lawrence and Karen Kushner; Full-color illus. by Dawn W. Majewski* A gentle way for young children to explore how God is with us every day, in every way. Abridged from *Because Nothing Looks Like God*.
5 x 5, 24 pp, Board Book, Full-color illus., 978-1-893361-17-1 **$7.99** *For ages 0–4*

What Does God Look Like? (A Board Book)
by Lawrence and Karen Kushner; Full-color illus. by Dawn W. Majewski
A simple way for young children to explore the ways that we "see" God. Abridged from *Because Nothing Looks Like God*.
5 x 5, 24 pp, Board Book, Full-color illus., 978-1-893361-23-2 **$7.99** *For ages 0–4*

How Does God Make Things Happen? (A Board Book)
by Lawrence and Karen Kushner; Full-color illus. by Dawn W. Majewski
A charming invitation for young children to explore how God makes things happen in our world. Abridged from *Because Nothing Looks Like God*.
5 x 5, 24 pp, Board Book, Full-color illus., 978-1-893361-24-9 **$7.99** *For ages 0–4*

What Is God's Name? (A Board Book)
by Sandy Eisenberg Sasso; Full-color illus. by Phoebe Stone
Everyone and everything in the world has a name. What is God's name? Abridged from the award-winning *In God's Name*.
5 x 5, 24 pp, Board Book, Full-color illus., 978-1-893361-10-2 **$7.99** *For ages 0–4*

Naamah, Noah's Wife (A Board Book)
by Sandy Eisenberg Sasso; Full-color illus. by Bethanne Andersen
We know the story of Noah, but what about Naamah, Noah's wife? This beautiful book will help you and your child explore the spirituality of this ancient story.
5 x 5, 24 pp, Board Book, Full-color illus., 978-1-893361-56-0 **$7.99** *For ages 0–4*

Or phone, fax, mail or e-mail to: SKYLIGHT PATHS Publishing
An imprint of Turner Publishing Company
4507 Charlotte Avenue • Suite 100 • Nashville, TN 37209
Tel: (615) 255-2665 • www.skylightpaths.com
rices subject to change.

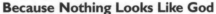

Adam and Eve's First Sunset: God's New Day
by Sandy Eisenberg Sasso; Full-color illus. by Joani Keller Rothenberg
9 x 12, 32 pp, Full-color illus., HC, 978-1-58023-177-0 **$17.95** *For ages 4 & up (a Jewish Lights book)*

Because Nothing Looks Like God
by Lawrence and Karen Kushner; Full-color illus. by Dawn W. Majewski
Real-life examples of happiness and sadness introduce children to the possibilities of spiritual life. 11 x 8½, 32 pp, HC, Full-color illus., 978-1-58023-092-6 **$17.99**
For ages 4 & up (a Jewish Lights book)

Also available: **Teacher's Guide,** 8½ x 11, 22 pp, PB, 978-1-58023-140-4 **$6.95** *For ages 5–8*

Becoming Me: A Story of Creation
by Martin Boroson; Full-color illus. by Christopher Gilvan-Cartwright
Told in the personal "voice" of the Creator, a story about creation and relationship that is about each one of us.
8 x 10, 32 pp, Full-color illus., HC, 978-1-893361-11-9 **$16.95** *For ages 4 & up*

But God Remembered: Stories of Women from Creation to the
Promised Land   *by Sandy Eisenberg Sasso; Full-color illus. by Bethanne Andersen*
A fascinating collection of four different stories of women only briefly mentioned in biblical tradition and religious texts. 9 x 12, 32 pp, Quality PB, Full-color illus., 978-1-58023-372-9 **$8.99** *For ages 8 & up (a Jewish Lights book)*

Cain & Abel: Finding the Fruits of Peace
by Sandy Eisenberg Sasso; Full-color illus. by Joani Keller Rothenberg
A sensitive recasting of the ancient tale shows we have the power to deal with anger in positive ways. "Editor's Choice"—American Library Association's *Booklist*
9 x 12, 32 pp, HC, Full-color illus., 978-1-58023-123-7 **$16.95** *For ages 5 & up (a Jewish Lights book)*

Does God Hear My Prayer?
by August Gold; Full-color photos by Diane Hardy Waller
Introduces preschoolers and young readers to prayer and how it helps them express their own emotions. 10 x 8½, 32 pp, Quality PB, Full-color photo illus., 978-1-59473-102-0 **$8.99**

The 11th Commandment: Wisdom from Our Children *by The Children of America*
"If there were an Eleventh Commandment, what would it be?" Children of many religious denominations across America answer this question—in their own drawings and words. "A rare book of spiritual celebration for all people, of all ages, for all time." —*Bookviews*
8 x 10, 48 pp, HC, Full-color illus., 978-1-879045-46-0 **$16.95** *For all ages (a Jewish Lights book)*

For Heaven's Sake   *by Sandy Eisenberg Sasso; Full-color illus. by Kathryn Kunz Finney*
Everyone talked about heaven: "Thank heavens." "Heaven forbid." "For heaven's sake, Isaiah." But no one would say what heaven was or how to find it. So Isaiah decides to find out, by seeking answers from many different people.
9 x 12, 32 pp, HC, Full-color illus., 978-1-58023-054-4 **$16.95** *For ages 4 & up (a Jewish Lights book)*

God in Between   *by Sandy Eisenberg Sasso; Full-color illus. by Sally Sweetland*
A magical, mythical tale that teaches that God can be found where we are.
9 x 12, 32 pp, HC, Full-color illus., 978-1-879045-86-6 **$16.95** *For ages 4 & up (a Jewish Lights book)*

God's Paintbrush: Special 10th Anniversary Edition
Invites children of all faiths and backgrounds to encounter God through moments in their own lives. 11 x 8½, 32 pp, Full-color illus., HC, 978-1-58023-195-4 **$17.95** *For ages 4 & up*

Also available: **God's Paintbrush Teacher's Guide** 8½ x 11, 32 pp, PB, 978-1-879045-57-6 **$8.95**

God's Paintbrush Celebration Kit
A Spiritual Activity Kit for Teachers and Students of All Faiths, All Backgrounds
Additional activity sheets available:
8-Student Activity Sheet Pack (40 sheets/5 sessions), 978-1-58023-058-2 **$19.95**
Single-Student Activity Sheet Pack (5 sessions), 978-1-58023-059-9 **$3.95**

Children's Spiritual Biography

Ten Amazing People
And How They Changed the World
by Maura D. Shaw; Foreword by Dr. Robert Coles
Full-color illus. by Stephen Marchesi

For ages 7 & up

Black Elk • Dorothy Day • Malcolm X • Mahatma Gandhi • Martin Luther King, Jr. • Mother Teresa • Janusz Korczak • Desmond Tutu • Thich Nhat Hanh • Albert Schweitzer

This vivid, inspirational and authoritative book will open new possibilities for children by telling the stories of how ten of the past century's greatest leaders changed the world in important ways.

8½ x 11, 48 pp, HC, Full-color illus., 978-1-893361-47-8 **$17.95**
For ages 7 & up

Spiritual Biographies for Young People—For ages 7 and up

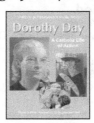
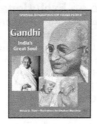
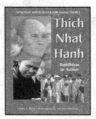

Black Elk: Native American Man of Spirit
by Maura D. Shaw; Full-color illus. by Stephen Marchesi
Through historically accurate illustrations and photos, inspiring age-appropriate activities and Black Elk's own words, this colorful biography introduces children to a remarkable person who ensured that the traditions and beliefs of his people would not be forgotten.
6¾ x 8¾, 32 pp, HC, Full-color and b/w illus., 978-1-59473-043-6 **$12.99**

Dorothy Day: A Catholic Life of Action
by Maura D. Shaw; Full-color illus. by Stephen Marchesi
Introduces children to one of the most inspiring women of the twentieth century, a down-to-earth spiritual leader who saw the presence of God in every person she met. Includes practical activities, a timeline and a list of important words to know.
6¾ x 8¾, 32 pp, HC, Full-color illus., 978-1-59473-011-5 **$12.99**

Gandhi: India's Great Soul
by Maura D. Shaw; Full-color illus. by Stephen Marchesi
There are a number of biographies of Gandhi written for young readers, but this is the only one that balances a simple text with illustrations, photographs, and activities that encourage children and adults to talk about how to make changes happen without violence. Introduces children to important concepts of freedom, equality and justice among people of all backgrounds and religions.
6¾ x 8¾, 32 pp, HC, Full-color illus., 978-1-893361-91-1 **$12.95**

Thich Nhat Hanh: Buddhism in Action
by Maura D. Shaw; Full-color illus. by Stephen Marchesi
Warm illustrations, photos, age-appropriate activities and Thich Nhat Hanh's own poems introduce a great man to children in a way they can understand and enjoy. Includes a list of important Buddhist words to know.
6¾ x 8¾, 32 pp, HC, Full-color illus., 978-1-893361-87-4 **$12.95**

Prayer / Meditation

Sacred Attention: A Spiritual Practice for Finding God in the Moment
by Margaret D. McGee
Framed on the Christian liturgical year, this inspiring guide explores ways to develop a practice of attention as a means of talking—and listening—to God.
6 x 9, 144 pp, HC, 978-1-59473-232-4 **$19.99**

Women Pray: Voices through the Ages, from Many Faiths, Cultures and Traditions
Edited and with Introductions by Monica Furlong
5 x 7¼, 256 pp, Quality PB, 978-1-59473-071-9 **$15.99**

Women of Color Pray: Voices of Strength, Faith, Healing, Hope and Courage *Edited and with Introductions by Christal M. Jackson*
Through these prayers, poetry, lyrics, meditations and affirmations, you will share in the strong and undeniable connection women of color share with God.
5 x 7¼, 208 pp, Quality PB, 978-1-59473-077-1 **$15.99**

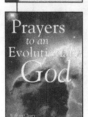

Secrets of Prayer: A Multifaith Guide to Creating Personal Prayer in Your Life *by Nancy Corcoran, CSJ*
This compelling, multifaith guidebook offers you companionship and encouragement on the journey to a healthy prayer life. 6 x 9, 160 pp, Quality PB, 978-1-59473-215-7 **$16.99**

Prayers to an Evolutionary God
by William Cleary; Afterword by Diarmuid O'Murchu
Inspired by the spiritual and scientific teachings of Diarmuid O'Murchu and Teilhard de Chardin, reveals that religion and science can be combined to create an expanding view of the universe—an evolutionary faith.
6 x 9, 208 pp, HC, 978-1-59473-006-1 **$21.99**

The Art of Public Prayer: Not for Clergy Only *by Lawrence A. Hoffman*
6 x 9, 288 pp, Quality PB, 978-1-893361-06-5 **$18.99**

A Heart of Stillness: A Complete Guide to Learning the Art of Meditation
by David A. Cooper 5½ x 8½, 272 pp, Quality PB, 978-1-893361-03-4 **$16.95**

Meditation without Gurus: A Guide to the Heart of Practice
by Clark Strand 5½ x 8½, 192 pp, Quality PB, 978-1-893361-93-5 **$16.95**

Praying with Our Hands: 21 Practices of Embodied Prayer from the World's Spiritual Traditions *by Jon M. Sweeney; Photographs by Jennifer J. Wilson; Foreword by Mother Tessa Bielecki; Afterword by Taitetsu Unno, PhD*
8 x 8, 96 pp, 22 duotone photos, Quality PB, 978-1-893361-16-4 **$16.95**

Silence, Simplicity & Solitude: A Complete Guide to Spiritual Retreat at Home
by David A. Cooper 5½ x 8½, 336 pp, Quality PB, 978-1-893361-04-1 **$16.95**

Three Gates to Meditation Practice: A Personal Journey into Sufism, Buddhism, and Judaism *by David A. Cooper* 5½ x 8½, 240 pp, Quality PB, 978-1-893361-22-5 **$16.95**

Prayer / M. Basil Pennington, OCSO

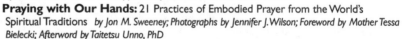

Finding Grace at the Center, 3rd Ed.: The Beginning of Centering Prayer *with Thomas Keating, OCSO, and Thomas E. Clarke, SJ; Foreword by Rev. Cynthia Bourgeault, PhD*
A practical guide to a simple and beautiful form of meditative prayer.
5 x 7¼, 128 pp, Quality PB, 978-1-59473-182-2 **$12.99**

The Monks of Mount Athos: A Western Monk's Extraordinary Spiritual Journey on Eastern Holy Ground *Foreword by Archimandrite Dionysios*
Explores the landscape, the monastic communities, and the food of Athos.
6 x 9, 256 pp, 10+ b/w drawings, Quality PB, 978-1-893361-78-2 **$18.95**

Psalms: A Spiritual Commentary *Illustrations by Phillip Ratner*
Reflections on some of the most beloved passages from the Bible's most widely read book. 6 x 9, 176 pp, 24 full-page b/w illus., Quality PB, 978-1-59473-234-8 **$16.99**
HC, 978-1-59473-141-9 **$19.99**

The Song of Songs: A Spiritual Commentary *Illustrations by Phillip Ratner*
Explore the Bible's most challenging mystical text.
6 x 9, 160 pp, 14 b/w illus., Quality PB, 978-1-59473-235-3 **$16.99**; HC, 978-1-59473-004-7 **$19.99**

Spirituality of the Seasons

Autumn: A Spiritual Biography of the Season
Edited by Gary Schmidt and Susan M. Felch; Illustrations by Mary Azarian
Rejoice in autumn as a time of preparation and reflection. Includes Wendell Berry, David James Duncan, Robert Frost, A. Bartlett Giamatti, E. B. White, P. D. James, Julian of Norwich, Garret Keizer, Tracy Kidder, Anne Lamott, May Sarton.
6 x 9, 320 pp, 5 b/w illus., Quality PB, 978-1-59473-118-1 **$18.99**

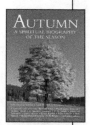

Spring: A Spiritual Biography of the Season
Edited by Gary Schmidt and Susan M. Felch; Illustrations by Mary Azarian
Explore the gentle unfurling of spring and reflect on how nature celebrates rebirth and renewal. Includes Jane Kenyon, Lucy Larcom, Harry Thurston, Nathaniel Hawthorne, Noel Perrin, Annie Dillard, Martha Ballard, Barbara Kingsolver, Dorothy Wordsworth, Donald Hall, David Brill, Lionel Basney, Isak Dinesen, Paul Laurence Dunbar. 6 x 9, 352 pp, 6 b/w illus., Quality PB, 978-1-59473-246-1 **$18.99**

Summer: A Spiritual Biography of the Season
Edited by Gary Schmidt and Susan M. Felch; Illustrations by Barry Moser
"A sumptuous banquet.... These selections lift up an exquisite wholeness found within an everyday sophistication."— ★ *Publishers Weekly* starred review
Includes Anne Lamott, Luci Shaw, Ray Bradbury, Richard Selzer, Thomas Lynch, Walt Whitman, Carl Sandburg, Sherman Alexie, Madeleine L'Engle, Jamaica Kincaid.
6 x 9, 304 pp, 5 b/w illus., Quality PB, 978-1-59473-183-9 **$18.99**
HC, 978-1-59473-083-2 **$21.99**

Winter: A Spiritual Biography of the Season
Edited by Gary Schmidt and Susan M. Felch; Illustrations by Barry Moser
"This outstanding anthology features top-flight nature and spirituality writers on the fierce, inexorable season of winter.... Remarkably lively and warm, despite the icy subject." — ★ *Publishers Weekly* starred review
Includes Will Campbell, Rachel Carson, Annie Dillard, Donald Hall, Ron Hansen, Jane Kenyon, Jamaica Kincaid, Barry Lopez, Kathleen Norris, John Updike, E. B. White.
6 x 9, 288 pp, 6 b/w illus., Deluxe PB w/flaps, 978-1-893361-92-8 **$18.95**
HC, 978-1-893361-53-9 **$21.95**

Spirituality / Animal Companions

Blessing the Animals: Prayers and Ceremonies to Celebrate God's Creatures, Wild and Tame *Edited by Lynn L. Caruso* 5¼ x 7¼, 256 pp, Quality PB, 978-1-59473-253-9 **$15.99**

Remembering My Pet: A Kid's Own Spiritual Workbook for When a Pet Dies
by Nechama Liss-Levinson, PhD, and Rev. Molly Phinney Baskette, MDiv; Foreword by Lynn L. Caruso
8 x 10, 48 pp, 2-color text, HC, 978-1-59473-221-3 **$16.99**

What Animals Can Teach Us about Spirituality: Inspiring Lessons from Wild and Tame Creatures *by Diana L. Guerrero* 6 x 9, 176 pp, Quality PB, 978-1-893361-84-3 **$16.95**

Spirituality—A Week Inside

Come and Sit: A Week Inside Meditation Centers
by Marcia Z. Nelson; Foreword by Wayne Teasdale
6 x 9, 224 pp, b/w photos, Quality PB, 978-1-893361-35-5 **$16.95**

Lighting the Lamp of Wisdom: A Week Inside a Yoga Ashram
by John Ittner; Foreword by Dr. David Frawley
6 x 9, 192 pp, 10+ b/w photos, Quality PB, 978-1-893361-52-2 **$15.95**

Making a Heart for God: A Week Inside a Catholic Monastery
by Dianne Aprile; Foreword by Brother Patrick Hart, OCSO
6 x 9, 224 pp, b/w photos, Quality PB, 978-1-893361-49-2 **$16.95**

Waking Up: A Week Inside a Zen Monastery
by Jack Maguire; Foreword by John Daido Loori, Roshi
6 x 9, 224 pp, b/w photos, Quality PB, 978-1-893361-55-3 **$16.95**; HC, 978-1-893361-13-3 **$21.95**

Spiritual Poetry—The Mystic Poets

Experience these mystic poets as you never have before. Each beautiful, compact book includes: a brief introduction to the poet's time and place; a summary of the major themes of the poet's mysticism and religious tradition; essential selections from the poet's most important works; and an appreciative preface by a contemporary spiritual writer.

Hafiz
The Mystic Poets
Preface by Ibrahim Gamard

Hafiz is known throughout the world as Persia's greatest poet, with sales of his poems in Iran today only surpassed by those of the Qur'an itself. His probing and joyful verse speaks to people from all backgrounds who long to taste and feel divine love and experience harmony with all living things.
5 x 7¼, 144 pp, HC, 978-1-59473-009-2 **$16.99**

Hopkins
The Mystic Poets
Preface by Rev. Thomas Ryan, CSP

Gerard Manley Hopkins, Christian mystical poet, is beloved for his use of fresh language and startling metaphors to describe the world around him. Although his verse is lovely, beneath the surface lies a searching soul, wrestling with and yearning for God.
5 x 7¼, 112 pp, HC, 978-1-59473-010-8 **$16.99**

Tagore
The Mystic Poets
Preface by Swami Adiswarananda

Rabindranath Tagore is often considered the "Shakespeare" of modern India. A great mystic, Tagore was the teacher of W. B. Yeats and Robert Frost, the close friend of Albert Einstein and Mahatma Gandhi, and the winner of the Nobel Prize for Literature. This beautiful sampling of Tagore's two most important works, *The Gardener* and *Gitanjali,* offers a glimpse into his spiritual vision that has inspired people around the world.
5 x 7¼, 144 pp, HC, 978-1-59473-008-5 **$16.99**

Whitman
The Mystic Poets
Preface by Gary David Comstock

Walt Whitman was the most innovative and influential poet of the nineteenth century. This beautiful sampling of Whitman's most important poetry from *Leaves of Grass,* and selections from his prose writings, offers a glimpse into the spiritual side of his most radical themes—love for country, love for others, and love of Self.
5 x 7¼, 192 pp, HC, 978-1-59473-041-2 **$16.99**

Journeys of Simplicity
Traveling Light with Thomas Merton, Bashō,
Edward Abbey, Annie Dillard & Others

Invites you to consider a more graceful way of traveling through life. Use the included journal pages (in PB only) to help you get started on your own spiritual journey.

by Philip Harnden
5 x 7¼, 144 pp, Quality PB, 978-1-59473-181-5 **$12.99**
128 pp, HC, 978-1-893361-76-8 **$16.95**

Spiritual Practice

Soul Fire: Accessing Your Creativity *by Rev. Thomas Ryan, CSP*
Shows you how to cultivate your creative spirit as a way to encourage personal growth.
6 x 9, 160 pp, Quality PB, 978-1-59473-243-0 **$16.99**

Running—The Sacred Art: Preparing to Practice
by Dr. Warren A. Kay; Foreword by Kristin Armstrong
Examines how your daily run can enrich your spiritual life.
5½ x 8½, 160 pp, Quality PB, 978-1-59473-227-0 **$16.99**

Hospitality—The Sacred Art: Discovering the Hidden Spiritual Power
of Invitation and Welcome *by Rev. Nanette Sawyer; Foreword by Rev. Dirk Ficca*
Explores how this ancient spiritual practice can transform your relationships.
5½ x 8½, 192 pp, Quality PB, 978-1-59473-228-7 **$16.99**

Thanking & Blessing—The Sacred Art: Spiritual Vitality through
Gratefulness *by Jay Marshall, PhD; Foreword by Philip Gulley*
Offers practical tips for uncovering the blessed wonder in our lives—even in trying circumstances. 5½ x 8½, 176 pp, Quality PB, 978-1-59473-231-7 **$16.99**

Everyday Herbs in Spiritual Life: A Guide to Many Practices
by Michael J. Caduto; Foreword by Rosemary Gladstar Explores the power of herbs.
7 x 9, 208 pp, 21 b/w illustrations, Quality PB, 978-1-59473-174-7 **$16.99**

Divining the Body: Reclaim the Holiness of Your Physical Self *by Jan Phillips*
8 x 8, 256 pp, Quality PB, 978-1-59473-080-1 **$16.99**

Finding Time for the Timeless: Spirituality in the Workweek
by John McQuiston II Simple stories show you how refocus your daily life.
5½ x 6¾, 208 pp, HC, 978-1-59473-035-1 **$17.99**

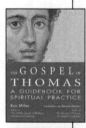

The Gospel of Thomas: A Guidebook for Spiritual Practice
by Ron Miller; Translations by Stevan Davies
6 x 9, 160 pp, Quality PB, 978-1-59473-047-4 **$14.99**

Earth, Water, Fire, and Air: Essential Ways of Connecting to Spirit
by Cait Johnson 6 x 9, 224 pp, HC, 978-1-893361-65-2 **$19.95**

Labyrinths from the Outside In: Walking to Spiritual Insight—A Beginner's Guide
by Donna Schaper and Carole Ann Camp
6 x 9, 208 pp, b/w illus. and photos, Quality PB, 978-1-893361-18-8 **$16.95**

Practicing the Sacred Art of Listening: A Guide to Enrich Your Relationships
and Kindle Your Spiritual Life—The Listening Center Workshop
by Kay Lindahl 8 x 8, 176 pp, Quality PB, 978-1-893361-85-0 **$16.95**

Releasing the Creative Spirit: Unleash the Creativity in Your Life
by Dan Wakefield 7 x 10, 256 pp, Quality PB, 978-1-893361-36-2 **$16.95**

The Sacred Art of Bowing: Preparing to Practice
by Andi Young 5½ x 8½, 128 pp, b/w illus., Quality PB, 978-1-893361-82-9 **$14.95**

The Sacred Art of Chant: Preparing to Practice
by Ana Hernández 5½ x 8½, 192 pp, Quality PB, 978-1-59473-036-8 **$15.99**

The Sacred Art of Fasting: Preparing to Practice
by Thomas Ryan, CSP 5½ x 8½, 192 pp, Quality PB, 978-1-59473-078-8 **$15.99**

The Sacred Art of Forgiveness: Forgiving Ourselves and Others through God's Grace
by Marcia Ford 8 x 8, 176 pp, Quality PB, 978-1-59473-175-4 **$16.99**

The Sacred Art of Listening: Forty Reflections for Cultivating a Spiritual Practice
by Kay Lindahl; Illustrations by Amy Schnapper
8 x 8, 160 pp, b/w illus., Quality PB, 978-1-893361-44-7 **$16.99**

The Sacred Art of Lovingkindness: Preparing to Practice
by Rabbi Rami Shapiro; Foreword by Marcia Ford 5½ x 8½, 176 pp, Quality PB, 978-1-59473-151-8
$16.99

Sacred Speech: A Practical Guide for Keeping Spirit in Your Speech
by Rev. Donna Schaper 6 x 9, 176 pp, Quality PB, 978-1-59473-068-9 **$15.99**
HC, 978-1-893361-74-4 **$21.95**

Spirituality

Next to Godliness: Finding the Sacred in Housekeeping
Edited and with Introductions by Alice Peck
Offers new perspectives on how we can reach out for the Divine.
6 x 9, 224 pp, Quality PB, 978-1-59473-214-0 **$19.99**

Bread, Body, Spirit: Finding the Sacred in Food
Edited and with Introductions by Alice Peck
Explores how food feeds our faith. 6 x 9, 224 pp, Quality PB, 978-1-59473-242-3 **$19.99**

Renewal in the Wilderness: A Spiritual Guide to Connecting with God in the Natural World *by John Lionberger*
Reveals the power of experiencing God's presence in many variations of the natural world. 6 x 9, 176 pp, b/w photos, Quality PB, 978-1-59473-219-5 **$16.99**

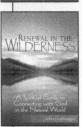

Honoring Motherhood: Prayers, Ceremonies and Blessings
Edited and with Introductions by Lynn L. Caruso
Journey through the seasons of motherhood. 5 x 7¼, 272 pp, HC, 978-1-59473-239-3 **$19.99**

Soul Fire: Accessing Your Creativity *by Rev. Thomas Ryan, CSP*
Learn to cultivate your creative spirit. 6 x 9, 160 pp, Quality PB, 978-1-59473-243-0 **$16.99**

Technology & Spirituality: How the Information Revolution Affects Our Spiritual Lives *by Stephen K. Spyker* 6 x 9, 176 pp, HC, 978-1-59473-218-8 **$19.99**

Money and the Way of Wisdom: Insights from the Book of Proverbs
by Timothy J. Sandoval, PhD 6 x 9, 192 pp, Quality PB, 978-1-59473-245-4 **$16.99**

Awakening the Spirit, Inspiring the Soul
30 Stories of Interspiritual Discovery in the Community of Faiths
Edited by Brother Wayne Teasdale and Martha Howard, MD; Foreword by Joan Borysenko, PhD
6 x 9, 224 pp, HC, 978-1-59473-039-9 **$21.99**

Creating a Spiritual Retirement: A Guide to the Unseen Possibilities in Our Lives
by Molly Srode 6 x 9, 208 pp, b/w photos, Quality PB, 978-1-59473-050-4 **$14.99**
HC, 978-1-893361-75-1 **$19.95**

Finding Hope: Cultivating God's Gift of a Hopeful Spirit
by Marcia Ford 8 x 8, 200 pp, Quality PB, 978-1-59473-211-9 **$16.99**

The Geography of Faith: Underground Conversations on Religious, Political and Social Change *by Daniel Berrigan and Robert Coles* 6 x 9, 224 pp, Quality PB, 978-1-893361-40-9 **$16.95**

Jewish Spirituality: A Brief Introduction for Christians *by Lawrence Kushner*
5½ x 8½, 112 pp, Quality PB, 978-1-58023-150-3 **$12.95** *(a Jewish Lights book)*

Journeys of Simplicity: Traveling Light with Thomas Merton, Bashō, Edward Abbey, Annie Dillard & Others *by Philip Harnden*
5 x 7¼, 144 pp, Quality PB, 978-1-59473-181-5 **$12.99** 128 pp, HC, 978-1-893361-76-8 **$16.95**

Keeping Spiritual Balance As We Grow Older: More than 65 Creative Ways to Use Purpose, Prayer, and the Power of Spirit to Build a Meaningful Retirement
by Molly and Bernie Srode 8 x 8, 224 pp, Quality PB, 978-1-59473-042-9 **$16.99**

Spirituality 101: The Indispensable Guide to Keeping—or Finding—Your Spiritual Life on Campus *by Harriet L. Schwartz, with contributions from college students at nearly thirty campuses across the United States* 6 x 9, 272 pp, Quality PB, 978-1-59473-000-9 **$16.99**

Spiritually Incorrect: Finding God in All the *Wrong* Places *by Dan Wakefield; Illus. by Marian DelVecchio* 5½ x 8½, 192 pp, b/w illus., Quality PB, 978-1-59473-137-2 **$15.99**

Spiritual Manifestos: Visions for Renewed Religious Life in America from Young Spiritual Leaders of Many Faiths *Edited by Niles Elliot Goldstein; Preface by Martin E. Marty*
6 x 9, 256 pp, HC, 978-1-893361-09-6 **$21.95**

A Walk with Four Spiritual Guides: Krishna, Buddha, Jesus, and Ramakrishna
by Andrew Harvey 5½ x 8½, 192 pp, 10 b/w photos & illus., Quality PB, 978-1-59473-138-9 **$15.99**

What Matters: Spiritual Nourishment for Head and Heart
by Frederick Franck 5 x 7¼, 128 pp, 50+ b/w illus., HC, 978-1-59473-013-9 **$16.99**

Who Is My God?, 2nd Edition: An Innovative Guide to Finding Your Spiritual Identity
Created by the Editors at SkyLight Paths 6 x 9, 160 pp, Quality PB, 978-1-59473-014-6 **$15.99**

Spirituality & Crafts

The Knitting Way
A Guide to Spiritual Self-Discovery
by Linda Skolnik and Janice MacDaniels
Examines how you can explore and strengthen your spiritual life through knitting.
7 x 9, 240 pp, Quality PB, b/w photographs, 978-1-59473-079-5 **$16.99**

The Scrapbooking Journey
A Hands-On Guide to Spiritual Discovery
by Cory Richardson-Lauve; Foreword by Stacy Julian
Reveals how this craft can become a practice used to deepen and shape your life.
7 x 9, 176 pp, Quality PB, 8-page full-color insert, plus b/w photographs
978-1-59473-216-4 **$18.99**

The Painting Path
Embodying Spiritual Discovery through Yoga, Brush and Color
by Linda Novick; Foreword by Richard Segalman
Explores the divine connection you can experience through creativity.
7 x 9, 208 pp, 8-page full-color insert, plus b/w photographs
Quality PB, 978-1-59473-226-3 **$18.99**

The Quilting Path
A Guide to Spiritual Discovery through Fabric, Thread and Kabbalah
by Louise Silk
Explores how to cultivate personal growth through quilt making.
7 x 9, 192 pp, Quality PB, b/w photographs and illustrations, 978-1-59473-206-5 **$16.99**

Contemplative Crochet
A Hands-On Guide for Interlocking Faith and Craft
by Cindy Crandall-Frazier; Foreword by Linda Skolnik
Illuminates the spiritual lessons you can learn through crocheting.
7 x 9, 208 pp, b/w photographs, Quality PB, 978-1-59473-238-6 **$16.99**

Kabbalah / Enneagram
(from Jewish Lights Publishing)

God in Your Body: Kabbalah, Mindfulness and Embodied Spiritual Practice
by Jay Michaelson 6 x 9, Quality PB Original, 978-1-58023-304-0 **$18.99**

Cast in God's Image: Discover Your Personality Type Using the Enneagram and Kabbalah
by Rabbi Howard A. Addison 7 x 9, 176 pp, Quality PB, 978-1-58023-124-4 **$16.95**

Ehyeh: A Kabbalah for Tomorrow *by Dr. Arthur Green*
6 x 9, 224 pp, Quality PB, 978-1-58023-213-5 **$16.99**

The Enneagram and Kabbalah, 2nd Edition: Reading Your Soul
by Rabbi Howard A. Addison 6 x 9, 192 pp, Quality PB, 978-1-58023-229-6 **$16.99**

The Gift of Kabbalah: Discovering the Secrets of Heaven, Renewing Your Life on Earth
by Tamar Frankiel, PhD 6 x 9, 256 pp, Quality PB, 978-1-58023-141-1 **$16.95**
HC, 978-1-58023-108-4 **$21.95**

Kabbalah: A Brief Introduction for Christians
by Tamar Frankiel, PhD 5½ x 8½, 176 pp, Quality PB, 978-1-58023-303-3 **$16.99**

Zohar: Annotated & Explained *Translation and Annotation by Dr. Daniel C. Matt*
Foreword by Andrew Harvey 5½ x 8½, 176 pp, Quality PB, 978-1-893361-51-5 **$15.99**
(a SkyLight Paths book)

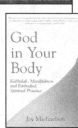

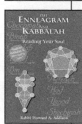

About SKYLIGHT PATHS Publishing

SkyLight Paths Publishing is creating a place where people of different spiritual traditions come together for challenge and inspiration, a place where we can help each other understand the mystery that lies at the heart of our existence.

Through spirituality, our religious beliefs are increasingly becoming a part of our lives—rather than *apart* from our lives. While many of us may be more interested than ever in spiritual growth, we may be less firmly planted in traditional religion. Yet, we do want to deepen our relationship to the sacred, to learn from our own as well as from other faith traditions, and to practice in new ways.

SkyLight Paths sees both believers and seekers as a community that increasingly transcends traditional boundaries of religion and denomination—people wanting to learn from each other, *walking together, finding the way.*

For your information and convenience, at the back of this book we have provided a list of other SkyLight Paths books you might find interesting and useful. They cover the following subjects:

Buddhism / Zen	Global Spiritual	Monasticism
Catholicism	Perspectives	Mysticism
Children's Books	Gnosticism	Poetry
Christianity	Hinduism /	Prayer
Comparative	Vedanta	Religious Etiquette
Religion	Inspiration	Retirement
Current Events	Islam / Sufism	Spiritual Biography
Earth-Based	Judaism	Spiritual Direction
Spirituality	Kabbalah	Spirituality
Enneagram	Meditation	Women's Interest
	Midrash Fiction	Worship

Or phone, fax, mail or e-mail to: SKYLIGHT PATHS Publishing
An imprint of Turner Publishing Company
4507 Charlotte Avenue • Suite 100 • Nashville, TN 37209
Tel: (615) 255-2665 • www.skylightpaths.com
rices subject to change.